I AM
ENOUGH.

HANAH SMITH

Juliana —
you are an incredible
force. Never doubt your
power or your immense
impact on people.
with gratitude
and love,
Hanah

ISBN 979-8-9873413-2-2 (hardcover)
ISBN 979-8-9873413-1-5 (paperback)
ISBN 979-8-9873413-0-8 (ebook)

For Sarah,
for myself,
and for all those who may see themselves in this story.

CONTENTS

RESOURCES

Thank you.

I start each day with words of gratitude, so it only feels right to begin my book the same way.

First, thank *you* for picking up this book. Thank you for spending time with me, my experiences, and lessons learned. If my story feels familiar to your own, thank you for being curious about where you're at in life and for having the courage to examine if what you've got is what you want *or* if it's time for a change.

Thank you, Colin. Thank you for being my true partner, my fiercest ally, and my home. Thank you for the unending support and encouragement you've shown me through this process and every day of our lives together. Thank you for the space and grace to explore my passions, work on me, and to create without any expectations except that I be true to myself. Thank you for the many coffee and writing dates, walks in the woods, and workshopping sessions while I talked things out. Through it all you encouraged me like no other. The depth of my gratitude is only exceeded by the depth of my love.

Thank you, Mom for your example of a strong and independent woman not afraid to go after what she wants and take big risks. Thank you for being introspective and showing me what it looks like to openly examine your past and present. Thank you for teaching me to listen to my heart and make emotionally informed decisions, and for all the wise words and life lessons you'll see peppered throughout these pages. You have the kindest heart, and you lift everyone around you.

Thank you to my Dad and Stepmom for being the first ones to show me what taking a break and changing careers could look like. Remembering the leap you took has helped me immensely in times where I felt scared and thought "Oh god, what am I doing? Can I do this? Will I land on my feet?" Thank you for leading by example in too many ways to name here. You taught me that it is the practical things done deliberately over many years that make the big, exciting moves possible. The beautiful combination of your curiosity, heart, determination, and logic brain are alive and well in me.

Thank you all — my three parents — for giving me the internal foundation, drive, and fortitude I needed to fly the nest and build my own, and now to rebuild.

Thank you to my Mother- and Father-in-law for raising an incredible human — three, actually! — and for your love, support, understanding, and encouragement as we have both navigated big life changes.

Thank you to my Stepdad. Though you showed up later in my life, I am always thankful for the unending love and support you show for the H women.

To my extended family, particularly the incredible women in my life (Grandma Bonnie, Debbie, Patty, Grandma Reata & Wendi): thank you for showing up for yourselves and sharing your stories with me. Thank you for being honest with me about your challenges, joys, and life lessons from the time I was little. I got to learn and grow through you, and I am deeply grateful for your vulnerability and intimacy, and your examples of love and strength.

To Sarah, my chosen sister and soulmate. I'm endlessly proud of you and the life you're creating for yourself. Thank you for being my person these 20+ years. It's a rare gift to have someone who knows where I came from *and* shares and celebrates where I'm going. Forever your hype woman.

Jenni, you are a beautiful human and I'm lucky to call you my dear friend and confidante. You are a force in business and deserve only the best.

To the incredible colleagues turned friends who have touched my life and been a critical part of my professional and personal journey for more than a decade — C, C, L, M, K, M, A & B — thank you. We've been through so much together and it warms my heart to no end to see you all writing your next chapters.

To those I've been lucky enough to coach and mentor: I'm so proud of you. Being a part of your lives and growth was and is one of my greatest joys and an absolute privilege. T & P: you were lights in my life when things got darkest.

Thank you, Beth, for your candor and for listening with an open heart when I needed help getting out of my own way. The space to be my true and highest self is a rare gift.

Thank you to the female influences I've never met but who have shared their stories with such honesty and vulnerability that it touched my soul and encouraged me to do the same: Brené Brown, Glennon Doyle, Sonya Renee Taylor, and Abby Wambach. These past three years of evolution wouldn't have been the same without you.

The many hours spent writing this book were also supported by the musical stylings of Taylor Swift, Tori Amos, Whitney Houston, and HAIM; the Palette Community (particularly my fellow redhead and tour de force, Marcella); and the incredibly nice baristas at Kru Coffee in Saratoga Springs, NY.

I gave myself
a chance
to be truly
and deeply
happy

SETTING MY INTENTION FOR OUR TIME TOGETHER

It's funny, for the last five years of my career (and probably more) I would say that the most common question I've asked people is: "What's the goal?" I work(ed) in public relations and the question was to be sure that (1) there was a clear end game for whatever communications campaign or initiative we were about to embark on and (2) everyone involved could get clear on and aligned with the same goal as our "North Star." What surprised me was how often people wanted to jump into doing the thing before getting clear on why they were doing the thing, and to what end.

This is me getting clear on the goal. I'm setting my intention for this book and our time together so that you and I are both clear on what this is — and what this isn't.

I am writing this book first and foremost for me. It is the thing I feel called to do and that I know I would regret if I didn't do it. I would regret not getting my thoughts, feelings, and ideas onto the page.

I am writing this book for those — however few or many — that may see themselves in these pages.

I am writing for the people who may have been called to make a change but ignored the whispering (or screaming) voice inside them. I believe we don't talk enough about making big changes in our lives and what that takes mentally, emotionally, and financially.

I don't have it all figured out. (It's OK to not have it all figured out!) But I did give myself a chance to be truly and deeply happy.

I can't make any promises about what's next — for me or for any readers of this book. What I can promise is that I will share my story with you with complete honesty and vulnerability. I believe that's what we need more of in this world to feel less alone, and, hopefully, to be informed and empowered to make change.

An important disclaimer:
My experience is that of a 37-year-old, white, heterosexual, cisgender woman. Woman is a key part of my identity as that is how the world has related to me in life and in business and treated me accordingly. I grew up in a middle-class family in two (very) different homes as the only child to divorced parents. I have been with my partner, Colin, for 19 years and married for 7. We do not have children. That is not my calling or his. We have two cats that occupy much of our conversation and iCloud photo storage.

My upbringing and lifestyle have been anything but "traditional," but I think it's important that you, my dear reader, know some broad strokes about me upfront for context.

I do not purport to represent any perspectives in here except my own. Everyone is unique. This is just me, sharing my story and my truth.

The voice inside me screamed: If you die tomorrow, you will die with regret.

APRIL 2018

There I was on the floor of my apartment, sobbing. Full, deep, rock you to your core sobbing. The kind where you're not sure what noises you're making, or if they're even coming from you. Is that me? Or is that a caged animal trying to get out? In that moment both statements felt true.

It was a few days after my Great Grandmother died, and the sadness and anger I felt were bubbling up at random times. That day, the feelings came at me while I was folding laundry. At first, I sat on my bed to cry. Then I slowly made my way to the floor because I wanted to feel something solid under my feet. I *needed* something solid under the weight of my body and all the emotions it carried. She and I were very close and losing her was a massive blow.

She was also the third family member I'd lost in almost as many months. My Great Uncle had passed in January 2018 and my paternal Grandfather "Grandaddy Smith" passed on in February 2018.

None of them ever met, but I'd like to think that they would have gotten along. They all worked hard, were mentally sharp until the day they died, had a glimmer in their eye for adventure, and didn't suffer fools. Real salt of the earth. All of them lived full lives, rich with love.

I was profoundly and deeply sad. I wondered how I even had any tears left after all the crying. But as I sat there on the floor, there was a voice inside me that was louder than my grief:

"If you die tomorrow, you will die with regret."

It could not have been clearer. The voice inside my head was screaming at me to let me know that if I continued on my current path, I would die with regrets over the way I was living my life — or, rather, not living it.

Four more people I loved and admired would die that year. Each person was an inspiration to live better. Each death was a reminder that if I didn't make changes I would regret it, and I would have wasted this one, precious life.

Time to go.

NOVEMBER 2020

It's Friday the thirteenth and today I gave notice. I gave notice during a pandemic and, shall we say, a 'bumpy' economy. My head keeps telling me I should be more nervous or even scared but I am so incredibly calm. I know this is the right move. I know that if I stay, no one will be getting the best of me — least of all me! — and no one deserves that.

Before calling or video chatting my coworkers to tell them the news, I close my eyes and recite the following in my own version of a quick meditation:

> "May you and I be at peace and
> may we both part in gratitude.
> I am grateful for the time, the opportunities, the lessons
> and the many wonderful and deeply caring people
> I met along the way.
> I want nothing more than for they and I to be left whole
> as we part ways."

For those close to me my news is no surprise. For others it seems genuinely shocking, but everyone understands and all the conversations I have that day go very well. We reminisce, we laugh a bit, and we cry a bit, but through it all my conviction never wavers.

When I walk out of my home office around 6:30 that night, I am severely dehydrated from all the talking/crying/laughing and my husband, Colin asks how I'm feeling.

"Really good."

"You sound SO calm. Throughout all of those calls you sounded, and still sound So. Calm." He could hear all the calls from the living room.

"I am," <deep breath> "because I know it in my bones that this is the right move."

A few more deep breaths and a pregnant pause later: "HOLY SHIT! THIS IS REAL."

We opened a bottle of champagne, and the rest of the night was pretty much spent smiling from ear to ear, shaking my head, and continuing to say "Wow, that happened" and "I'm just so excited!"

It was such a relief to finally speak this truth — my truth — to my colleagues, people whom I respected and cared about so much.

Then I was
free.
(Sort of...)

FEBRUARY 2021

Today, Friday, February twelfth, in the year of our goddess twenty twenty-one, I wrapped up and left my job of nearly nine years. After three months of transition planning, coaching, lots of brain dumps, and regular check-in conversations with all my colleagues, the day had finally come to leave it all behind.

In my final week, I sent and received many heartfelt emails. There was a small group Zoom goodbye during which I said a few words to let my closest colleagues know how much they meant to me and how much I had cherished our time together. I cried. Some other folks on the line did too. And then it was done.

It's a strange and inglorious sensation to not have an in-person goodbye party or gathering of some kind. In these unprecedented times you simply close out your email, as you would any other Friday, and never return.

Then I was free. Sort of...

Hi!
I'm Hanah with
one 'n'

A LITTLE BIT ABOUT ME

(...before I was that puddle on the floor of my apartment)

I was born in 1985 in Little Rock, Arkansas to two deeply thoughtful and caring humans. Shortly thereafter, their paths took them in different directions and when I was about one-and-a-half, my parents divorced after seven years of marriage. My dad remarried when I was three-and-a-half years old so in my memory I've always had three parents.

Until I was 11 years old, I lived with my mom and visited my dad and stepmom during the summer and every other holiday. Then, halfway through fifth grade, I switched to go live with my dad and stepmom. It was incredibly hard to leave my mom and only see her summers and holidays, but it felt like something I had to do. I had this internal calling: I needed to get to know my dad better and understand that "half" of me.

Between my parents I lived in nine states (Arkansas, California, Texas, New York, Indiana, Pennsylvania,

Maryland, Michigan, and Vermont) and two countries (the U.S. and the Netherlands).

No matter which house I was in, my parents modeled and instilled in me the value of hard work to achieve the things I wanted out of life.

About my parents...

I come from hardy stock as they say. In middle school, my mom babysat and mowed lawns. Then, when she was 14 years old, she lied on her first job application so she could start working in fast food restaurants. My dad also began taking on jobs around his neighborhood when he was in middle school. The first thing he can remember doing is helping construction workers salvage bricks from demolished houses. (My favorite part of that story though is that he found a tiny grey kitten in some of the rubble one day, saved it, and named it Concrete. So cute, right?)

It wasn't expected that either my mom or dad would go to college, but they were both the first and only ones in their families to go to and graduate college. They worked the whole time to pay their tuition and the bills. They both take pride in the fact that their first home was a trailer and that they used to figure out how to feed themselves on $10 a week. They told me this story more than once when I started working and thinking about college. I think they wanted me to know that the middle class lives they both enjoyed by the time I was a teenager didn't just happen and shouldn't be taken for granted. I think it was also a way of setting expectations that things would not simply be given to me, by them or the world.

My stepmom's upbringing was a bit different, but she had similar beliefs about hard work. However, for her, higher education was always an expectation. Her dad was the first in his family to go to college, working and paying his way through school to get a PhD. He was determined to get educated and create the best possible life for his wife and children — breaking the cycle of what he had seen in his family. The stories I heard most often from that side of my family were about the value of higher education and applying yourself as the foundation of a better life.

All these lived experiences and beliefs about hard work and education funneled down to me. My parents loved me deeply, and encouraged and supported me, but I also felt the pressure — real or self-inflicted — of the high hopes and expectations they had for their only child.

"You better work b*tch" ~Britney Spears

When I was 10 years old, I wanted this big, fluffy stuffed animal raccoon from Toys 'R' Us. It was $40. Instead of buying the raccoon for me, my mom said that she would invest in me if I was to take on an entrepreneurial venture and make the money myself.

I decided to sell Yo-Yo balloons. If you were a kid in the mid 90s to early aughts you may remember these. They were essentially half-filled, extra strong water balloons tied to a bungee string with a loop at the end for your finger, thus creating the Yo-Yo. They were $50 for a pack of 40. I liked the balloons and that was a price my mom was willing to pay to invest in my "business."

We lived in Texas at the time and there was a big parade coming up in downtown Houston where I thought I could sell them. My mom helped me with the math to understand that to pay her back and buy my raccoon, I would have to sell each Yo-Yo balloon for at least $2.25. I decided to sell them for $5 per balloon because 10-year-old me rarely saw people with change, but I had seen people pay for things with $5 bills. Solid logic if you ask me.

I filled and assembled all the balloons and put them in one of those personal wire grocery carts with wheels. Then, with my mom behind me, I went up and down the downtown Houston parade route touting my wares.

I was so scared at first. It felt like being on stage while I was shouting "Yo-Yo balloons, five dollars! Get your Yo-Yo balloons!" But the more I did it, the less scary it was.

All told, I sold half my inventory and made $100! I was so excited that I got enough money to pay back my mom and, most importantly, get that raccoon. I cherished that thing because I had worked hard for it. It felt good to earn it versus the fleeting high of being given something. I was good to all my stuffed animals, but the raccoon held a place of honor.

I didn't realize it at the time, but there were a couple lessons I learned and stories I told myself about this experience:

1) It feels good to *earn* something.
2) It feels good to work through challenges, even when they seem scary and much bigger than you.
3) Making money takes hard work.
4) It feels good to reward yourself with *things*.

When I was 11, I started earning an allowance. I got $8 per week for doing the dishes every night. Plus-ups were possible if I wanted to do more chores: $2 for vacuuming, $5 for mowing the lawn, and some amount I can't remember for cleaning the bathrooms. That was my money to do with as I wanted.

When I was 13 and 14, I needed something to do for the summer but couldn't legally work yet, so my mom set me up with some local volunteer positions. First, I worked as a teacher's assistant at a literacy camp, then I helped file papers and work the front desk at our local Habitat for Humanity.

When I was 15, I started my first paying job. If you visited Hershey Park in the summer of 2000, you may have seen my smiling face at the water cart, the slushie and fried dough gazebo, or the kosher hot dog hut. No matter what the position, I was determined to do the best job possible. My efforts earned me the coveted title of "Employee 2000." <Flips hair> Pretty cool, right? It was just a fancy way of saying employee of the month, but I was super proud to get that on my name tag. There wasn't any extra money that came with it though. It was basically like using a gold star as a motivation tool. But dammit, I got it.

Once I got my driver's license at age 16, I got a job as a waitress. I worked weddings and large parties on Friday and Saturday nights and did the Sunday Brunch shift at the same facility.

We lived comfortably and I didn't *need* to work, but it was something I felt I should do. I also wanted the extra spending money for shoes, clothes, and going out with friends.

I had a Type A personality and tied my worth to how hard I worked, what grades I got, and what — and how much — I achieved.

In school, I did everything I could to get good grades. I also pushed myself to be "good at everything" and take on the hardest classes. I took honors English, math, biology, political science, and language classes. It didn't matter if I was passionate about a subject, I was laser focused on excelling. I was disappointed in myself for getting grades less than anything in the 90-100 range. And the low 90s were only really "OK" for me in my hardest subject: college level calculus.

I ran cross-country in the fall and played rugby in the spring while also practicing for and performing in the spring musicals. For a few years I also worked chorus into that schedule.

In case you're wondering, I didn't sleep much. I remember watching Leno and Conan late at night long after my parents had gone to bed because I wanted the company while I stayed up working on my homework. I didn't do drugs to keep this schedule either or partake in drugs or drinking of any kind. At the time I thought it might ruin a potential political career after seeing what happened to former President Bill Clinton when he said he "didn't inhale." If I was going to go to law school and become Vermont's second female governor, by golly I needed to keep a spotless record. Ohhh, young me.

When I was 18, I went straight from high school to Northeastern University in Boston. I started off as a Political Science major but switched to Journalism[1] by the end of my first year.

Because Northeastern is a co-op school where students are required to get on the job experience, students typically alternate spending one semester in class and the next semester working. This means that they usually graduate in five years. I pushed through to graduate in four years because all four of my internships

---

[1] Thank you, Professors Carlene Hempel and Dan Kennedy. Your classes lit a fire in me.

in the communications field were unpaid or minimally paid ($10 per day) and I was eager to start my career. For extra spending money, I worked as a hostess at a popular local restaurant, Legal Seafoods.

It was in college that I first discovered coffee and began to dabble in the art of working in coffee shops late at night to get work done. Once the coffee shops closed, I could also be found in the library pulling all-nighters. Sleep was less important to me than maintaining a high GPA.

The point is, I was accustomed to working hard, long hours with perfection being the expectation long before I joined the workforce.

In May 2007, I graduated with my Bachelor's in Journalism, and double minors in Communications and Political Science. I was 22 and ready to "hit the ground running" as the cliché goes. I graduated on Saturday, May 5 and started work at my first full-time job on Monday, May 7.

VP by 30

WORKING GIRL

(But sadly, no Melanie, Sigourney, or Joan)

At my first full-time job the set working hours were 8:30 a.m.-5:30 p.m. but I showed up early every day at 7:45 or 8 a.m. at the latest and didn't leave until at least 6 or 6:30 p.m. I worked in public relations, which meant I also needed to have a handle on the news of the day before getting to the office. I'd wake up at 5:45 a.m., do a media scan on my personal laptop, then pick up *The Boston Globe* on my way into work so I could read it on the T. I would also check my work email at home just to be sure I didn't miss anything from a boss or client. I remember being excited when I got my first work BlackBerry so that I could more easily check email and stay on top of work after hours.

My starting salary was $32,000. The work culture was sink or swim and I worked relatively nonstop to try to swim the hardest and fastest. My hustle paid off and I got three promotions in three years and worked my way up to a $52,000 annual salary. It was a harsh training ground

29

for my first full-time job, and I cried in the bathroom more times than I'd like to admit. *But* the job also challenged me in ways that I enjoyed, and I was given a lot of opportunities to take big swings, even at a young age, once I had "proven myself."

During my time there, I was fortunate enough to have one of the owners take an interest in me and act as my supervisor and mentor. I don't take for granted that a strong female leader who had started and built her own business was spending her valuable time with me. I think she was willing to invest in me because it was clear how much I had invested and was willing to invest in the company and our clients' success.

I also deeply valued that I was part of a small but mighty collection of women. Even though the way we were treated by some in charge could be borderline abusive[2], we had each other, and I felt like we could get through anything because we were all in it together.

---

[2] To be clear, what I'm talking about here is verbal abuse. The best definition I can find for this behavior in the *workplace* is from Section 12950.1 of California's Government Code: "Abusive conduct may include repeated infliction of verbal abuse, such as the use of derogatory remarks, insults, and epithets, verbal or physical conduct that a reasonable person would find threatening, intimidating, or humiliating, or the gratuitous sabotage or undermining of a person's work performance."

Was I once told "You should have stopped before you started" when responding reasonably to a direct question? Yes. Was I called stupid for not seeing what was in fact an invisible calendar appointment? Also, yes. It was trying to work for someone with a Jekyll and Hyde personality where one day you were the favorite and the next you could do nothing right. But hey, verbal insults were still a step up from the last job I had before graduating college where an intern had a phone thrown at them and where I once hid under a desk with my laptop so that I could continue working while the boss looked for someone to yell at for a scratch on the wall.

Even with the bad behavior at my first full-time job, because of the potential for upward mobility and this big goal I had set for myself of making VP by 30, I honestly think I might have stayed at that job longer if it weren't for one bad hire and one unattended salary list.

A few years into my tenure, they hired a man, let's call him "LL" for life lesson. They hired LL to fill a position two levels above me. He had a lot of connections that higher-ups thought would help with new business, but at a basic level he didn't know what he was doing when it came to public relations. I always want to give new hires a fair chance and I understand that there's a learning curve with any job, so I helped him at first. Unfortunately, it quickly became apparent that he wasn't there to be a collaborative colleague. He would call me into his office, close the door so no one would overhear our conversations, and ask what I thought we should be doing for our clients. Then he would pass off my ideas as his own. One time, after asking for help with solving yet another client crisis, he even had the nerve to say to me "I don't know what I'd do without you. I really don't know what I'm doing." Thanks for being honest I guess, *but* also stop stealing my ideas and pay me accordingly if I'm doing *your* job.

Then, one night when I was working late, I went to get something off the printer and saw another document that had been left sitting there: the list of everyone's salaries. LL made almost double my salary.

I was incensed and moved to act. Ahead of my next regular check-in with my supervisor, I prepared unemotional talking points[3] laying out my ask, i.e., what's

---

[3] I put a lot of pressure on myself to have unemotional conversations when it comes to business dealings (and other areas of my life) because I don't want to be written off as an "emotional woman" and have everything I say be tuned out and invalidated.

the problem, what is the impact on my work/the business, and what's my proposed solution.

I made sure the conversation we had was very measured with concrete examples. There were multiple incidents of him taking exactly what I had said/created/written and passing it off as his own. I asked that the issue be addressed directly with him or that I work with other client team managers. I had helped him and given him plenty of time and chances to be a good colleague and now I needed someone above him and me to step in.

I was treated as if I was overreacting. I took a breath and calmly let them know that if things didn't change with him, I would start looking for other jobs.

Shortly thereafter, I was scheduled for my annual review. Emboldened by seeing the other salary information, and angry that someone who took my ideas and "only" worked 9-5 was getting paid almost twice as much, I decided to do some math. I went back through all my timesheets from the past year and added up all my hours. My salary was supposed to be commensurate with a 40-hour work week with occasional spikes when there was a major project or deadline. On average, I worked 60 hours per week. Yes, I worked hard and did extra work to get ahead, but when faced with the numbers I could see that for a full year I had effectively worked 20 hours a week for free.

Doing the math

Here's a fun exercise. Take your annual salary and divide it by the number of business hours in a year. Say you're making a $50,000 gross annual salary. Divide that by 2080 (52 weeks per year x 40 hours per week = 2080 business hours). That means you have an hourly wage of ~$24 if you work "normal business hours." Now, if you worked an average of 60 hours per week x 52 weeks that's a total of 3120 business hours. A $50,000 annual salary divided by 3120 business hours = ~$16 per hour. That means you're making ~$8 less per hour on average. It also means that if you had been paid for that time, you would have made an additional $24,960. Here's the math:

3120 hours worked

- 2080 avg. business hours

= 1040 hours

1040 hours x $24/hour = $24,960

Another way of thinking about it is that you gave your employer 26 weeks (1040 hours of time) FOR FREE. That's six months of work. Let that sink in. Half. Of. A. Year. that you weren't getting paid for.

In addition to calculating my total hours worked and the dollar value of that compared to my salary, I also came to the table with other important business numbers and bullet points, mainly:

- Revenue managed and revenue contributed through client renewals and/or new business;
- Number of staff managed, retained, developed, and promoted; and,
- Substantial staff and culture contributions.

I had an exemplary review. At the end of the discussion, they offered me a promotion (yay!) and a $2,000 increase in annual salary. It was an almost 4% raise, which did fall within the range of the 3-5% annual increases typical of a profitable business. That's nothing to sneeze at and I wasn't ungrateful for it. *However*, it was less than half the average 8-10% increase typical of a promotion in the industry.

When my boss asked me how I felt about it I got very quiet and then calmly said: "Honestly, it feels like a slap in the face."

I don't know where that came from. I was always honest but very measured, and I had just spoken with no filter. At that point in my career, I still very much skewed toward trying to smooth things over in tough conversations versus being comfortable with necessary discord and awkward silence.

And boy was this an awkward silence. But it was powerful because I didn't speak next. My boss was caught off guard and said they were sorry I felt that way but that there wasn't anything they could do. My next words were: "Thank you, you've given me a lot to consider."

At that point, I was the fifth longest standing employee in a firm of ~20 people, right after the owners and C-level folks. In a matter of six months, they had shown me that they valued the new guy over me and would allow his poor behavior to continue *and* that they weren't willing to pay me commensurate with industry standards and the value I added to the company.

In the next conversation I had with my supervisor, I said again how much I appreciated the kind words about my performance and the promotion in title. However, I reiterated that if things didn't change with LL or the salary offering, I would need to look elsewhere. I also shared that I wasn't trying to threaten anything or maneuver but that I wanted to be honest and upfront.

They were still surprised when I gave notice. <Stares directly at camera a la Jim Halpert>

I was willing to work long, hard hours when I knew that behavior and investment would eventually be rewarded. I couldn't allow myself to stay at a place where (1) I knew there was enough money to pay people fairly for a job well done, and (2) my good work, loyalty, and kindness weren't being rewarded and instead were being taken advantage of.

For my second job I decided to apply to a much larger company that would give me the opportunity to work on bigger accounts that were national versus regional in scale and where I could learn a different type of PR (corporate vs. public affairs and nonprofit focused). I also had a former colleague who had gone on to work for said big company and was singing their praises. I was only able to negotiate a $3,000 pay increase but the nearly lateral move was worth it to me to get out of my current situation, try something new, and build my skillset.

The people at my new job were very friendly and collaborative. There were a few characters, as there are in any company, but there were many more great examples of what inclusive and supportive leadership looks like.

They used more carrots than sticks to incentivize stellar work quality and client service.

As lovely as the team was and as much fun as I had working with major national brands, I continued to work long, hard hours. It was fine at first, but after a year I knew it wasn't going to be a fit for me long-term. If I was going to continue to put in that time and effort, I wanted to do that for organizations and causes close to my heart.

I didn't get a large pay increase or get promoted during the time I was at that job (not unexpected of a large company), but I did learn a valuable lesson about the type of work that I wanted to do. Importantly, I also got to see and experience many examples of positive and supportive leaders who still got the best out of themselves and their colleagues sans fear.[4]

In 2011, we moved from Boston to Maryland so that Colin, my then boyfriend (now husband) could go back to school.

---

[4] Nicholle, Amy, and Amelia — if you happen to be reading this, I hope you know what a positive impact you had on me during our time together. You brought it every day and I'm thankful to have worked with and for such incredibly smart, driven, and kind women.

For me, being in the DC area opened a whole new world of opportunities for work. Two former colleagues turned friends worked for a national PR firm that was far and away my top choice for a new job. I loved what they had to say about working there and I knew of no other firm like it that was working exclusively with nonprofits and foundations on positive social change.

I was also drawn to the leadership team, the opportunity to shape positive company culture and, hopefully, help build a team of happy people doing good work in the world. Those two colleagues turned friends had worked with me at my first job and, for their own reasons, they too wanted to create something different. They knew that you didn't have to create a culture of fear to get good work out of people. Other members of the leadership team had also come from PR firms that were less than stellar culturally speaking, and it felt like we had instant comradery there. We were all committed to not perpetuating bad behaviors.

In May of 2012 I started working at a company I was truly enamored with.

A page from my gratitude journal after my first week on the job.

This job felt like the big leagues. We were working on major issues including criminal justice reform, climate change, reproductive rights, and international development and disaster relief. The nonprofits and foundations we worked with were positively impacting people's lives on a large scale with multi-million-dollar community investments. And we were supporting changes to state and federal policy that could benefit generations well beyond ours.

I was excited by the work, and I felt a strong sense of belonging with the people on my team. It felt like we were all in it together. As a more senior person on a small team of what was then ~12 people, I also relished that I finally had a chance to put my own stamp on things: from making a big deal out of team wins and life events (usually celebrating with food or drinks), to investing in the much deeper interactions like 1:1 coaching and making sure people felt seen and heard. I wanted to give them all better than what I had "growing up" in PR.

I honestly believed I would stay at the firm until I was in my 40s or 50s before moving "in house" to work solely for one organization I was deeply passionate about. It still stings a bit that I thought our relationship would last decades. It's hard to let go of the things we once loved and that began so beautifully.

I truly loved my new job, or at least I think I did. I'm not sure if I loved it or if I was addicted to it. I had always fed off the fast-paced energy of a PR firm and the excitement of every day being different. Yes, you develop long-term communications plans, define strategy, and work toward goals but the news is a surprise every day, and if you're going to be good at your job you must react well in the moment. You have to be thoughtful, well informed, and have or know how to get answers quickly — and engage the people around you to act. I thrived on that kind of work and feeling like that kind of person.

I still worked long hours and my life was not my own. My phone and laptop were always with me, including nights, weekends, and on "vacation." I remember one Saturday I was trying on wedding dresses while coordinating a CNN interview with first responders in Nepal and relief organization leadership back in DC.

But I didn't see anything wrong with that. I felt like goddam Olivia Pope. "It's handled."

I kept it up because I was working for clients and causes I cared about, I had a great team, I was learning and growing, and I was pushing myself in new and interesting ways. I also knew that the promotion I had been working toward was within reach.

Remember what I said about that big goal I had set for myself? In my new position, I was 27 and one promotion away from being a Vice President.

I was
on top of
the world

SEPTEMBER 2015

My promotion is official. I knew it was in motion and I learned it had been approved by higher-ups in August but now it's been made public. My colleagues know and I get to openly celebrate: I'M A VICE PRES-I-DENT!!! I did it. I actually did it.

I'm 30 years old. I'm a Vice President. I'm about to marry my beloved partner of 12 years. And he's about to get a shot at his dream job! This is amazing. I also just learned that my most demanding accounts are slowing down in Q4, so I should be able to take time off without work for my honeymoon.

Everything is working out for Hanah Smith.

Coffee.
Wine.
Repeat.

2016

In 2015 I planned and executed a wedding for 150, hustled for a major promotion, and supported my partner in switching his career. I remember it as being one of the best years of my life. Turns out, it was also the calm before the storm.

I had been doing the job of a Vice President for at least a year before I got the title and raise, but for the next 18ish months I had full blown imposter syndrome (a phrase and condition I didn't even know about until I read the book *Lean In* in 2013). So, I did what any reasonable person would do: I hustled even harder because I wanted to prove — again! — that I belonged and that I still deserved the title.

In addition to that self-inflicted pressure in the workplace, in the spring of 2016 my colleagues and I were launching a new campaign that I was managing. It was high stakes, high visibility work for our largest client and it had me and a handful of colleagues working 12-

hour days on the regular. While challenging, it was meaningful work that I cared deeply about doing well.

As much as I cared though, it took a lot of effort to keep going and pushing through to get the work done because one of my client contacts was verbally abusive. I don't use this term lightly nor am I exaggerating. I looked up the definition while working with this person because of how poorly they treated me, my team, and other consultants. To protect my team (1) out of human decency and (2) so that they could continue to get all their work done, I took on the unhappy role of being this person's main contact, AKA acting as a corporate human shield and punching bag.

I made myself a martyr. What I should have done was stand up for myself and my team and bring the issue to higher-ups to address head-on.

I knew what was happening was wrong, but my first instinct was to compromise my wellbeing to make my coworkers and clients happy. I hadn't internalized yet that being a good leader wasn't about martyrdom — it was, and is, leading by example. Standing up for myself and the team would have given others an example of when and how to do that *and* given them "permission" to do the same for themselves in the future.

As it was, it was a daily struggle to keep doing my best work and to keep motivating those around me to do their best work when I couldn't predict when or why this person would go off on us. My computer monitor was literally covered in Post-it notes listing the behaviors, words, and phrases that had set this person off at some point. I kept them front and center on my desk so that I and my team could remember them all and not step on those landmines. That spring was the worst of it, but that unhealthy relationship would continue for another two years. I don't even want to know the volume of coffee and wine I consumed in my time working with that person.

In the background, I was managing a lot at home too. As soon as we returned from our honeymoon, Colin had to go to Air Traffic Control training for four months in Oklahoma City before moving to upstate New York where he got placed as a Controller at Albany Airport. I didn't know if my company would allow me to keep my job and work from New York but at the time we were willing to do whatever *the company* was OK with. Despite the hours, the biggest stressors at my job all felt like outside factors

— not internal issues — and I wanted to keep working there.

Thankfully, a few others at my company had moved for life events so there was openness to employee relocation and working from home, but it was very much the exception. Before moving, I was warned that working remotely could be detrimental to my future trajectory and upward mobility because of the value placed on in-office interactions. It was a risk I was willing to take to be with my family: my husband and our two cats.

After spending the first nine months of our marriage living apart, I was able to pack up all our belongings and move to New York to join him.

Imposter syndrome & proving that work from home is working

It never stops. To get promoted to Vice President, I had to prove that I was already doing the job. Once I got the promotion, I worked even harder to prove I could keep up with those who had already held the position for years longer than I had. Then, in the summer of 2016 I moved to upstate New York and began working out of a home office.

I was already the type of person that would have applied tremendous self-pressure to that situation. On top of that, a higher-up whose words carried tremendous weight told me outright that I should consider the move as a trial period and that it would be up to me to show that nothing was "lost" by working remotely.

I began work between 7-8 in the morning, took a break for dinner around 7 p.m. and then would be on email again between 8-9 p.m. I kept this schedule so that I could get ahead of the East Coast teams and be responsive to all the West Coast folks emailing later in the day.

As most have now experienced firsthand because of COVID, I was more productive during the hours I spent working from home because I didn't have the same level of in-office distractions and I wasn't losing time commuting — which had cost me anywhere from 45 min. to two hours each way depending on how the metro was feeling that day.

Still, I made the effort to show up in person, too. That year, I spent ~$2,000 of my own money travelling back to our core offices to be sure my presence was felt, and to put in quality face time with my teams, supervisees, and higher-ups. For the next two years (2017-2018) I personally spent ~$4,000 per year travelling to our multiple East and West Coast offices. I genuinely wanted to be present for my teams and supervisees, but I also didn't want to be "out of sight out mind" with higher-ups because of working from home.

No one asked me to spend my money that way and I don't blame them for my choices. But I wish I had valued my own time and money then the way I do now.

I made it work. But it wasn't sustainable...

I wish I knew
then
that it was
the beginning
of the end

2017

In the summer of 2017, I was blindsided by junior staff sharing a letter notifying management of their intent to vote on forming a union.

To be clear, I wasn't upset that my coworkers would organize! I 1000% support unions and the right to organize. Unions serve a critical function in the workforce to ensure fair, equitable pay and good working conditions and that's just at the most basic level. We also have unions to thank for the weekend and a myriad of other health care and leave benefits that most people now consider standard practice. Not to mention that part of my household's income and benefits, and Colin's working conditions are protected directly by the NATCA labor union. (Shoutout to the National Air Traffic Controllers Association — y'all are incredible).

What I was hurt and saddened by was the idea that people I had worked with for more than six years, people I was both personally and professionally close to, felt they had to work on something like this in secret and hadn't come to me or other managers to voice problems so that we could work on changes together.

Because of the example my mother had set for me growing up, I always valued and prioritized being an honest and empathetic leader. I often heard one or both sides of work conversations in the car, at home, or in her office. She would also share with me (before and after) the tough conversations she had to have at work when people weren't being treated fairly or weren't doing right by their colleagues or clients.

As a team manager, she wasn't one to force her idea of how things should be done. Instead, she would spend time (often lots of it) truly getting to know people, their strengths, concerns, interests, etc. so she could figure out how they worked best and help them shine. She worked at being fully present to whatever her coworkers, bosses, and employees were going through and how she could help them to do their best work, whether it was with her or not.

The number of times she helped coach people out and helped them find other jobs also speaks to how much she just wanted the best for people, whatever that journey looked like for them. I went to a lot of work functions with my mom and every time I met one of her colleagues, I was always struck by how effusive they were. "I just love your mom. She's the best!"

From those experiences, I internalized that deeply thoughtful and compassionate leadership wasn't easy but that all the extra time and energy — not just showing up and focusing on your own job — was more than worth it to have a positive impact on people's lives.

Because of what I had experienced in my internships and at my first job, once I was finally in a position of power and could shape policies and culture, I was determined to do better and make our workplace as supportive as possible.

I aimed to be the type of leader that people felt they could have candid conversations with and could count on to be honest, direct, and kind in return. I worked hard at being a strong advocate for my colleagues and empowering them to advocate for themselves, too.

I felt horrible thinking that people I cared about so deeply were hurting this badly. I felt shame trying to rack my brain for signs that I might have missed, or comments I may have dismissed. And I felt deeply hurt that people I felt so close to would send a legal notice instead of talking to me or others first so we could be partners in making change.

After that, our team fundamentally shifted. There were things we could no longer discuss openly, and trust was broken on both sides. Where once I felt in close collaboration and partnership with all my colleagues, in an instant I felt I could only trust and be open with a handful of them because of the literal legal lines that were drawn. It was the end of what I had known.

For the next year we all continued with our work while the union vote and subsequent bargaining agreement and contract negotiations took place. The process was messy at times, but I was grateful for it in the end. I had been so focused on our small 20-person division that I hadn't fully realized the discrepancies in pay, training, and treatment across all 150 employees.

The contract negotiation process also gave me a lot of exposure to other parts of the company and the other personalities, behaviors, and conflicting management styles that I had been shielded from up to that point.

In late 2018 the contract was finalized, and we began the process of effectively forming a new company where we no longer operated as relatively autonomous divisions and instead had to integrate and assimilate.

I had felt a deep connection to that team of 20. **Within the new leadership structure and larger reorg, I kept seeing ways in which I didn't fit.**

Work had been hard for a long time because of the long hours, the occasionally cruel client, and the external and internal pressures I felt. *But* I felt like I and we as a small team could survive anything when we were all in it together. I felt like I could face anything and deal with the unreasonable moments at work when bad stuff came at me from "out there." Now, with a waning sense of belonging, I felt more alone in the fight.

I shouldn't
have to
scream
to be heard.

BACK TO 2018

Have you ever screamed into a pillow? Not in *that* way, but when you're deeply angry or hurt. When I feel those kinds of emotions bubbling up inside me in a big way, I'll go into a room, close the door, hold a pillow to my face and scream out a good long and loud "MOTHER F*CKER!!!" You can also do this in parked car.

I did that more than a few times in 2018. But the scream that was the loudest was the one that never even left my body. It was that voice inside me screaming that I would die with regret.

I was a scene that day. As I mentioned, in April 2018 I was on the floor of my apartment, sobbing uncontrollably. I reached a depth of sadness and hurt I'd never felt before. Normally a very positive and upbeat person, I wondered when I would stop hurting.

I was personally and professionally drained.

My work hours and the intensity of work had consistently increased for four straight years. Hustle even harder to prove I deserve the VP promotion -> Keep my foot on the gas to prove I belonged in the position once promoted -> Work round the clock so no one can doubt my ability to work from home -> Pile on admin work to have a voice in the company reorganization and continue to (hopefully) positively shape company culture. And for the last two of those four years there was a client in my life that would email, call, or text at least once a day that was a mystery bag: you never knew when you were going to get kicked or complimented for the same quality and quantity of work.

Since starting the job in 2012, I had only taken one vacation that didn't include work email, calls, or texts. Add to that the heartbreak of losing seven people I knew and loved, one of whom passed way before their time. All told, it was a series of shocks to an overworked and worn-out system. But mostly it was a wakeup call.

The voice inside me was screaming and it terrified me, but I was and am so grateful for that alarm bell. Looking back, I know I would have heard that voice a lot sooner if I had ever stopped to listen. If I had ever stopped to ask myself what I needed and wanted — not just what my job, clients, colleagues, family, etc. wanted.

I wasn't proud of the person I had allowed myself to become, and I needed to make serious changes.

Why did I create that?

Whenever something upsetting would happen when I was growing up, say a fight with a friend, a scraped knee, or I was feeling left out, my mom would always ask me: "Why did you create that?"

Truth be told, when you're a kid, this question is a-nnoy-ing. You want to just be upset and be right about it. But the root of the question wasn't about blaming me for creating the bad thing. It was about personal accountability and taking back my power.

The question "Why did you create that?" forced me to take a deep breath, get quiet, and think about my actions and how I might be responsible for the situation. What role did I have in creating or allowing the upsetting thing to happen?

When I was eight, my mom and I lived in the Netherlands. Before moving back to the U.S., I got into a series of fights with my best friend, Kim. I became so frustrated that our last few months together were spent arguing. When I brought it up to my mom, she came at me with that dammed question again. But when I got still and allowed myself to think about it, I realized something:

Why did I create that? I thought it would be easier to say goodbye when I moved if I pushed Kim away.

How did I create that? I started fights to try and protect myself from the deeper hurt of leaving my best friend.

Once I realized what I was doing, I stopped bickering with her and instead got to fully enjoy our last few weeks together riding bikes, having sleepovers, and going to the candy store for licorice and 90210 trading cards (you know, typical 90s kid stuff). Saying goodbye still hurt, but it was better to have made the most of the time we did have together.

This question has guided me throughout my life. I've just modified it slightly. **I ask myself both why *and how* did I create that so that I can look at the emotion behind the action (why) and the action being taken (how). It's a powerful tool for accountability and taking back the reigns of my life (power).** If I created the thing, then I can also un-create it *or* create something entirely new.

Importantly, asking myself "Why did I create that?" does not mean that I take on *all* the responsibility of a bad situation or that I take on the responsibility of *every* situation. This is about taking a hard look at what I can control for, *not* carrying the weight of everything and everyone around me.

Asking "Why did I create that?" also does not mean that I skip over the parts of life where I feel hurt, mad, or angry. Whenever I am upset, I allow myself to be upset. I vent. I sometimes let out a primal scream in the car (God, that feels good). If I need a good cry, I pop on my headphones, play the Johnny Cash version of Hurt, and just let it all out.

I want to feel everything and not numb or suppress my emotions because feeling everything allows me to *process* the emotions, let them out, and figure out what's left over that actually needs to be dealt with.

In 2018 I was deeply unhappy but if *I* created that situation then *I* also had the power to change it and create something different.

I cried. I screamed. And then I began the process of having hard conversations with myself.

Why and how did I create this breakdown?
I didn't value my needs and desires and ignored myself in all the ways that mattered.

I took on too much at work. To get ahead I had always taken on more than could fit into a 40-hour work week. I put up very few boundaries with my coworkers, and those I did put up, I didn't do a good job of protecting and maintaining. "I'll be out but if you need anything urgently you can call or text!" I wasn't sharing enough responsibilities and was lying to myself that I could still "do it all," saying yes to new opportunities and responsibilities without shedding/transitioning old ones. I would get up early and work late into the night so that I could get my work done *and* be fully available to my teams, clients, and managers during normal business hours.

I didn't have a system for taking care of my body. I started the day with coffee and rarely ate breakfast. I would often skip lunch due to meetings and then dash into the kitchen or run out to the local salad and sandwich place any time between 1-4 p.m. (whenever I could find a break in meetings). Dinner was the only consistent meal I ate because cooking was (and still is) a stress reliever and creative outlet for me. But even then, at least once a week I was too exhausted to cook or think about what to make so we'd go out to dinner or get takeout. Once I started working from home in 2016, I spent most of the day inside, not getting fresh air or direct sunlight. I only went for walks or hikes or worked out on the weekends, if at all. But even that was tricky because the weekends were also occupied by getting groceries, doing the laundry, and cleaning.

I wasn't feeding my mind. I know that I get my best ideas from: reading books, magazines, and the Sunday paper; listening to podcasts; going to museums; participating in conferences/webinars/meetups that give me a chance to talk to new people and push or otherwise expand my thinking; and, taking long walks in the woods where I can let my mind wander. I rarely did these things and was constantly asking my brain to generate new ideas while feeding it scraps — literally and figuratively.

I prioritized others over myself. Do you know that song "Girl" by Tori Amos? There's a line in it that has always pierced my heart: *"She's been everybody else's girl, maybe someday she'll be her own."* Work came first and after that, I put Colin, family, and friends ahead of my needs every. time. Loving them meant making them happy first. Even when Colin repeatedly said, "Tell me what you need to create time and space for yourself," I rarely did.

I didn't say no to requests, and I didn't ask for help because a big part of my identity was that of a do it all perfectionist. ("It's fine, I've got it!") And I was always a "good girl" when it came to family and friends — a good daughter, homemaker, granddaughter, niece, sister-in-law, host, you name it. My Dad affectionately calls this the "Golden Retriever syndrome": it's when you smile and do everything you can to make your family happy.

I could see all the ways I wasn't valuing my time or wellbeing and I didn't blame those around me. I not only didn't set boundaries, but I also raised my hand for additional opportunities at work and with family. Why though? To prove I was the best? Prove I could do it all and keep up the façade of perfection?

When it came to making changes and creating something new though, I wasn't sure where to begin. It all felt overwhelming.

My body and that voice inside me were telling me what was wrong. I decided I needed to listen to them more to tell me what felt right.

What
energizes
me?

"There's no time." "I'm exhausted." "I can't." "Ugh, I have to get it up for work again. Is there a blue pill for that?"

All the things that I was giving my time to weren't things that I hated. I truly cared about the causes I worked on. I had some near and dear colleagues. I loved (and obviously still love) my family and friends and it's important to me to show up for them and enjoy whatever time we have together on this earth.

As with most things, there was no cut and dry "this is bad, and this is good." But the overwhelming *feeling* I had was that of being drained of energy. I wasn't doing or making enough time for the things that I felt energized and excited by.

I needed to listen to my body and figure out what it was that did and did not energize me.

A pros and cons list felt too simplistic. On its face, "long hours at the office" seems like it would go on the cons side. However, there are moments when projects that take a lot of time can also be incredibly energizing. I can recall multiple times in my life where I was working 60-hour weeks and I felt Alicia Keys level on fire. I felt so alive and energized by the work that I was doing *and* energized by how in sync my team was as we forwarded shared goals.

I wanted a better question for myself to help figure out what I was giving my energy to and what was — and wasn't — giving me energy in return. I decided that for a month I would keep track of everything I did at work and see how it made me feel with these two questions as my guide:

1) **What is energizing when I do it? What excites me, makes me feel inspired, or propels me forward?**
2) **What makes me feel drained, depleted of energy, or even angry?**

I focused on work first because it occupied most of my time and mental space. I wrote these questions at the top of a Word document that I kept open on my desktop. After every task and meeting I wrote down which column that activity/task fit into. Did I feel energized? Or did that activity feel like an energy drain? Sometimes activities were energy neutral. I didn't write those down because they neither took nor gave but felt like a necessary part of doing business. I did this for a month to capture the regular cycle of activities in my job (i.e., what happened weekly, every two weeks, and monthly) and get a well-rounded snapshot of what was and what wasn't working for me.

Some of the things that *energized* me at work:

- Coaching my direct supervisees. Anywhere from 1-4 hours per week I had the pleasure of talking 1:1 to incredible women I cared deeply about, working together to tackle problems, and discussing new ideas about our teams, the company and/or women in the workforce.
- Coaching women to talk to the press (aka media training) to help them tell their stories, boost their confidence about their experiences and expertise, and be sure they could protect themselves in public conversations. (Plus, all the last-minute calls, no matter the time of day, to give them a pep talk as needed before an interview and to celebrate them after the fact.)

- Deep learning on an issue, including reading books, magazines, journal articles, etc. and listening to podcasts and interviews that provided in depth and well-rounded perspectives on an issue. (But this was an activity I only had time to do on the weekends/personal time).
- Investing in our team through internal culture and policy work and systems development (e.g., training programs, fairness in staffing, bonus equity, internal communications, etc.) and seeing that pay off in the people around me and the ways they were better supported.

I was also energized by coming up with new campaign ideas and working with clients to help solve big problems. I relished being a part of long-term, sustainable change and the moments where we got to see the fruits of our labor. However, as is the nature of long-term work, the wins (understandably) took a while and weren't a frequent source of positive energy.

Things that *drained* my energy at work:

- Consistent undervaluing of internal culture, policy, and administrative work. Unpaid and undervalued work that was disproportionately done by and asked of women.
- The expectation of availability on email, Slack, and text. I still have a negative reaction to the classic Slack notification tone whenever it chimes because for years it felt like a petulant child constantly saying "Gimme! Gimme! Gimme!"
- General disrespect for time. For example, an email at 5:15 p.m. asking for something meaty to be reviewed before EOD, or a text message while I was out asking about something that was laid out in a "while I'm away" Google doc.
- Meetings with no clear goal or where I felt unnecessary. (Cliché but real and so. much. time.)

And, because of all the above, feeling like there's "never enough time" to do my own work and to generate new ideas as an individual and as a team leader.

From there, I looked at my list and identified:

- **What I had the power to change.**
- **What I needed other people's help with or action on to change.**
- **What, if anything, felt like it might never change or would require a bigger shift in the organization and/or leadership to make it change.**

Things I had the power to change, I took immediate action on.

Problem: Never feeling like I had enough time to do my own work.

Action: I blocked my calendar in the mornings so that I could do focused, creative, generating work when I knew my brain was the sharpest. I talked to my teams about it and let them know I would be off email, Slack, and text but they could call if they needed to reach me.

I also had some honest and tough conversations with direct reports where I saw an imbalance in responsibilities, i.e., where I had taken on too much or wasn't letting go of the reigns enough. I talked to them to (1) own my role in creating the imbalance, (2) understand their side of things, (3) figure out how we could transition responsibilities in a fair and supportive way, and (4) get a handle on what help and support they might need from others to ensure they didn't become overloaded and overworked either.

Problem: Being emailed 30 minutes before EOD to review something ASAP.

Action: I blocked a daily review period on my calendar and, for any needs outside of that, asked my teammates to block review time with me too. That way everyone could clearly see and plan for when to get me things for review depending on when they needed it back by. This held both me and them accountable to timelines and deadlines.

I also pulled back on the volume of deliverables I had been reviewing. Some things I had been reviewing out of habit but no longer needed my weigh in. Other deliverables were good growth opportunities for people on my team. I just needed to transfer ownership, remove myself from the process, and get out of their way.

Problem: Meetings with no clear goal or where I felt unnecessary.

Action: I reviewed all the meetings on my calendar to determine what I should still be a part of vs. where I could pull back and to see what we could outright cancel. There was so much I and my teams were doing out of habit and routine. Not being thoughtful and intentional about meetings and collaboration was a time suck and energy drain for everyone. I adjusted my schedule with colleagues and asked all meeting makers (the humans not the Outlook calendar request function) to add the following to every calendar appointment:

- Meeting goal and/or questions we need to answer
- What do attendees need to prepare to have a productive session?

We also worked on some team-wide guidelines together like striving for meeting free Fridays, scheduling shorter meetings, leaving 5-10 min. breaks in between calls for bathroom and water breaks, and not scheduling people for more than two hours in a row.

Problem: Consistent undervaluing of internal culture, policy, and administrative work.

Action: Such an easy fix! Just kidding. This was the hardest one to tackle because I had to separate my own feelings of wanting to invest in and help nurture people and culture. I wanted to do that kind of work, but I needed to narrow my commitments after years of (1) doing that work without the hours allotted for it (i.e., doing it on top of my core job responsibilities, usually on weekends) and (2) being repeatedly shown it was unpaid and undervalued labor. It wore me down.

In addition to the client work I was responsible for I was a leader or co-leader for many internal projects that I had initiated or raised my hand for. I needed to narrow in on what was most important to me and, otherwise, pass the torch to other team members or end the projects because they had served their purpose.

For each of the internal projects I wanted to transition, I took a hard look at the goals and what still needed to be accomplished and created a plan to help make that happen. I presented the plan to my supervisor, complete with my reasoning for why and how these projects should transition for the good of the company, *and* for the good of me and my time.

To proactively try and build in more time for rest and re-energizing, I looked at my vacation time and scheduled days off for the entire next year. I was inspired to do this because of Colin's work where people "bid" for all their guaranteed vacation time once a year (usually in the fall) so they can get all their time off on the books for the next calendar year. This forced me to think about my time in advance instead of expecting or hoping that as the year progressed, I'd somehow make time for vacations when things weren't too busy. Once I put the vacation days on the calendar, that time was protected. I could always decide not to use those vacation days, but if I didn't get them on the calendar in advance, I wouldn't be good about finding or taking time off. It was just too easy to make excuses about why I shouldn't or felt like I couldn't take the time.

The best part of making all these changes wasn't just getting more of my time back. My actions also gave others inspiration and "permission" to do the same with their time and calendars. **I think as colleagues and leaders we can often forget how much the respect we have for our own time and our behaviors and boundaries — or lack thereof — can affect others.**

Inspired by the changes I was able to make at work, and now becoming more in tune with what was giving me energy versus what was an energy drain, I turned my eye to what changes I could make at home.

Things that *energized* me at home included:

- Cooking. As much as I might feel drained at the end of the day and just want to plop down on the couch and order takeout, I knew that I would feel better after cooking dinner. Cooking was, and is, a creative outlet for me. Cooking allowed me the time to decompress from work by doing something physical and using my hands, senses, and a different part of my brain to come up with new dishes.

- Reading. I had always been a voracious reader growing up and love to get lost in books. When I was little, I used to lament to my mom that I only got to have the experience of being one person. Books allowed me to get into the minds and experiences of others.

- Going for walks in the woods and listening to podcasts. I loved the time I got to "spend" with Brené Brown, the HBR Women at Work crew, Ezra Klein, and Shankar Vedantam.

- Physical exercise I enjoyed like hiking, dance, and yoga.

There were also many other things that brought me joy and/or peace but I put this in a different category. For example, snuggling with my very fluffy rescue cat, Tuna, and hearing her purr brings me great joy. Staying in bed with my family on a Sunday morning brings me immense happiness and fills my heart with love. Those are lovely and necessary points of connection and moments of peace and rest that I relish. But, for me, those aren't the things that energize me and fuel my creativity. If I did too much of those things, I would stay on the couch and in bed for hours on end. I would not be inspired to go create or have the mental energy to create.

Things that *drained* me at home:
- Not doing enough of any of the above things.
- Watching too much Netflix to "tune out" of my life.
- Eating a bag of Cape Cod chips with French onion dip instead of cooking. You know, for emotional support.

Once I had a solid list of things that energized or drained me, I also made a list of the necessary activities that were just part of being a human in American society.

Mainly, groceries, laundry, and other home related chores.

For a long time, I had made excuses about how much time I had — or didn't have — to do things for myself.

To hold myself accountable for the situation I had created, I took a hard look at my time and how I was using it.

Math again

7 days a week x 24 hours per day = 168 hours

If I was getting 8 hours of sleep per night (we're talking ideal, OK?) that would be 56 hours of sleep per week.

168 - 56 = 112 non-sleeping hours per week

If I could take back my time at work and only work 9- to 10-hour days (45-50 hours per week) that would still leave me with a minimum of 62 non-sleeping non-work hours every week (112 non-sleeping hours - 50 work hours per week).

Weekend days are 13 hours long minimum if I allow myself to sleep in until 8 a.m. and go to bed early at 9 p.m.

One weekend day covers the necessities: roughly 3 hours for grocery shopping and weekly meal prep, 3 hours for starting/moving/folding laundry, and the rest for cleaning the house/misc. home chores and errands.

62 non-sleeping non-work hours - 26 weekend hours (13x2) = 36 hours per work week or ~7 hours per workday (36 hours per week divided by 5 days per week) of personal time.

7 hours per day - 1 hour to have breakfast, shower and get ready every morning = 6 hours

6 hours - 1 hour to prep and eat dinner every night = 5 hours every weekday

Rounding down to give myself conservative estimates, this math told me that *I could have at least 5 hours every weekday and 13 hours every weekend of "free time" to fill with activities that energized versus drained me.*

Doing the math forced me to account for all my personal time and allowed me to call bullshit on my perception that there was "never enough time."

To reclaim my time, I decided to start small. I chose just two things from my "feels energizing" list to add into my daily Monday to Friday routine: 30 minutes of any physical activity (walking, working out, yoga, stretching, or whatever felt good that day) and 30 minutes of reading every night. I also gave myself a general assignment of doing one outdoor walk/hike/something in nature every weekend.

To help keep myself accountable for making changes to my schedule I started to calendar out my personal life, too. I went so far as to calendar out my morning routine — including breakfast! — and my evening routine, including dinner and reading time. This helped me see where there was and wasn't free space and it helped me stick to a schedule not just for work but *for myself*. It also helped me set boundaries when new personal and/or professional requests came in because I wanted to maintain my schedule.

At least for a while, these changes worked and gave me some reprieve.

I was able to reclaim some time at work and at home. By leaning into what energized me *and* by shedding the things that drained me (i.e., things I thought I should be doing to be a good worker and a good girl) I also began forming basic healthy habits that supported my body and mind.

"Women have learned that we can be grateful for what we have while also demanding what we deserve."
~ Abby Wambach

GRATEFUL AND DEMANDING

Where were you in my 20s Abby?! I can clearly remember the first time I read Abby Wambach's remarks from her 2018 Barnard College commencement speech. Those words freed me.

I was extremely grateful for everything I had. Yet even with how hard I worked, and how much time, energy, and money I put into my job, I struggled to stand up for what I deserved. It felt as if the two were inherently contradictory. How can I be truly grateful for what I have *and* ask for more?

Reading Abby's words somehow gave me permission to hold both of these truths. I wrote "We can be grateful for what we have while demanding what we deserve" on a Post-it that lives on my desk to this day.

Were there things that could be better at my job? Absolutely. That's true of any workplace. But on the whole, I knew I had a lot to be grateful for.

At the most basic level, I was grateful to have a job. That's something I never took for granted, especially after seeing so many people get laid off in 2008, only a year after graduating college and entering the workforce. I was grateful to have steady income as well as vacation days, healthcare benefits, and 401K matching. I was grateful to have a job where I had been able to climb the ladder and earn enough power, influence, and respect to make positive changes in the workplace and the lives of others.

Even though the group was shrinking year over year, I still had a solid group of teammates (direct reports, peers, and leaders) whom I cherished, admired, and was inspired by. We were there for each other in good times and bad and we strived to bring out the best in one another.

I also truly loved what I worked on: criminal justice reform, gender equity and reproductive justice, climate change, public health, etc. It was hard and emotionally taxing work, but I loved being even a small part of the long-term, sustainable change happening on these issues. The organizations I worked with were incredible change agents and I loved getting to be their thought partner, putting our heads together to tackle some of the biggest issues of the day.

Wasn't that enough? With so much to be grateful for how could I push for more?

We can be grateful for what we have while demanding what we deserve.

Thank you, Abby.

In the spring of 2019, I was on track to be promoted to Senior Vice President. I was already doing the job and had checked all the boxes for promotion (at least all that existed up to that point).

However, before the review period, the goalposts changed. We had to hit our financial growth goals for the year *and* pull in some hefty additional revenue to justify an SVP promotion. Looking back at our historic earnings, I knew that kind of new revenue number had only been achieved once in the past decade. I raised the mathematically unrealistic and nearly unprecedented nature of this new rule with managers hoping that higher-ups would modify the additional revenue policy. With no immediate changes in sight, I was frustrated for a variety of reasons, but I held out hope that, given my strong numbers (revenue managed, renewed, and gained) and the mounting evidence of how I was already performing at the SVP level, the promotion would go through by the fall review period.

I didn't start looking for new jobs because I still wanted to make things work. Like I said, there was a lot to be grateful for. I also held out hope that the company would do right by me and that the new rule would be adjusted to reflect financial realities.

I not only held out hope, but I doubled down. The competitive, stubborn side of me said "I'll show you." I'll not only keep doing the job of SVP, but I'll get as much additional revenue as I can so that there's zero reason or excuse not to promote me.

WTF brain? I backslid and was regularly working 60–80 hours per week. It's hard to look back on the number of texts I sent saying "Please have dinner without me."

In the fall of 2019, the second review period of the year rolled around. Despite a strong year, nothing had changed. I didn't get promoted and more new metrics had been added to move the promotion goalposts even further.

<Deep breath> We can be grateful for what we have while demanding what we deserve.

In addition to Abby's words, I began to recall those of the soul-lighting Maya Angelou.

"When someone shows you who they are, believe them the first time."
~ Maya Angelou

It feels ungrateful to be in a stable job, making good money, and yet still asking for more. But I wasn't ungrateful. I recognized and outwardly acknowledged to my manager and other higher-ups how much good there was. I was very grateful for what I had. *AND* I deserved to have the title and compensation commensurate with the job I had been performing for nearly a year at that point. I had to hold and get comfortable with both truths in order to fight for myself and not feel guilty about asking for what I had earned. But it was also time to see the situation for what it was.

At one point in the ongoing promotion discussions, I was told/asked: "I don't know if I can get either of these approved but if you had to choose, what matters to you more, the money or the title?" I politely but firmly said "I shouldn't have to choose. I should have the title and compensation that are commensurate with the job I'm doing and have been doing for a year."

With no change in sight to these new rules and an open-ended potential promotion date, I needed to take a stand for myself.

I asked my manager point blank if they and others believed I was doing the job of a Senior Vice President and should be promoted.

Yes.

So, the only thing keeping me from being promoted is this new, higher revenue requirement?

Yes.

I was clear with my manager that, while I understood the businesses' prerogative to act in their own best interest with the new goalposts for promotion, I hoped they would understand that I needed to act in my own best interest as well.

I told my manager "I don't feel valued here." It hurt me to say it. I could feel the tension and pain behind those words balling up in my throat. It was hard to say it, but it was the truth. It stings like a mother not to feel appreciated by the place and people you've poured your time and energy into for nearly a decade. As much as I had to be grateful for, and as much as I wanted to stay for my clients and dearest colleagues, I couldn't continue to allow myself to be devalued. It wasn't right and I deserved better.

By the fall of 2019, I was deeply sad and disappointed. With no changes in sight, I let my manager know that I would need to begin looking for a new job. It wasn't said as a threat, I just felt the need to be transparent and continue to put my cards on the table for my own integrity. Thankfully, we had the kind of relationship where I could always be honest and direct.

I was cautious about the job search and not going for a "rebound" job because I was still feeling hurt. **I didn't want to run *from* the situation I was in — I wanted to run *toward* a new opportunity that would excite me.** I wanted to be intentional about what was next for me. To figure out what I wanted out of a new job, not just what I didn't want, I needed time and headspace; two things that were increasingly difficult to come by.

Thankfully, I had enough PTO banked (mostly from working through all my vacations...) to block out some three- and four-day weekends for myself. I was blocking time to build the life I wanted.

> *Sidebar: I have told other women in my life about this approach, and many (a) also have lots of unused vacation time (shocker!) and (b) have been able to set and keep the boundaries necessary to figure out what's next for them. They got the physical and mental space they needed to change their situation for the better either through job crafting, finding a new job, or building up what was their side business. One woman I know even took it a step further and was able to negotiate a sabbatical period with her employer. The time away allowed her to realize that she didn't want to leave the company, but she did want to create a new role for herself in a different division and she did!*

Unfortunately, this approach of blocking long weekends was unsuccessful for me for a few reasons:

1) It took a long time for me to decompress from the work week and get into a clear headspace. I wasn't able to close my laptop on Thursday night, put up a mental blockade, and not think about work until the following Monday.

2) I set but wouldn't consistently *enforce* boundaries for my time off when work requests came in.

3) I would get last minute requests late in the day before my day off that would bleed into the next day.

4) I would get texts from coworkers during my days off. My all-time favorite: a text I got asking if I had any issues with a vacation request that person had just submitted...for a trip that was months away.

Items 1 and 2 are totally on me and I own that. The coworker behavior in 3 and 4 made me frustrated and angry. It was important to me that my colleagues felt they could take time off when they needed it and weren't disturbed. Why couldn't I take one GD day?

The anger and frustration I felt just multiplied. In the immortal words of David Rose, it felt like "so many wrong things, one after the other, consecutively, in a row." I was putting in a full week's worth of work before taking a day off, but there was no actual break. It's strangely maddening when you keep trying to take just one full day off and it feels like the impossible dream because of constant interruptions.

I kept pushing, trying to make this approach work, but I kept meeting resistance. It became harder to decompress because I was low-level angry most of the time and I had my back up because I was basically waiting and expecting to be interrupted on days off. There was no room to explore and create what was next for me from a positive place, mentally or emotionally because I was so focused on the negative and trying to push against it.

I took a vacation in February 2020 that pushed me over the edge. It was the first weeklong non-family vacation Colin and I had taken since our honeymoon in 2015. In addition to comprehensive "While I'm out" google docs, I pre-emptively took two days "off" before our flight out to wrap up work and handle last-minute requests.

I still got texts on vacation. I was seething but I hid my feelings because I was tired of word vomiting my work problems on to my supportive partner who already didn't get enough of my time and attention. I didn't deserve that on vacation and neither did he.

Fuck this. I'm over it. Why hustle to make enough money to take vacations that you can't truly and fully enjoy or be present for? I had had enough of not being able to take undisturbed time away for myself.

After five months of trying to create space and maintain boundaries, it was clear that things weren't going to change at work. I had the option of staying mad and continuing to try and force the outcome I wanted, *or* I could accept the situation for what it was and put my energy toward creating something entirely new for myself.

I had to be honest with myself. I wasn't making any real progress on figuring out what was next for me and my career, much less taking the steps necessary to line that up. I began to get comfortable with the idea that I probably needed to leave my job so that I could actually take the time I needed to figure out what was next.

I tentatively planned to give notice after the spring review period (March 2020). I didn't have a firm plan yet and, in my heart of hearts, I think I was still holding on to a small sliver of hope that something might change and surprise me during the review period.

Well, I think we all know what happened next. I made plans. God laughed.

By the end of March 2020, it was back to basics. I was just grateful to have a job, especially one that I could do (and had been doing) from home.

In a surprising twist, the beginning of the pandemic gave me renewed hope and energy at work. We were all thrown into the same terrifying boat (life raft?) and the sense of camaraderie and care that emerged across colleagues and clients was truly heartwarming. Our clients also had a direct hand in helping to save lives and providing for people in the face of a social safety net that was so desperately lacking. As tumultuous as everything was in the world, the idea that I could help my clients help others *energized me.*

By the fall though, that little flame of renewed hope and energy was completely snuffed out.

As with any relationship, and as many experienced in 2020, dark times have a way of exposing the problems that were always bubbling under the surface. Trying experiences can bring people together and forge their bonds in fire or they can cause an irreparable rift.

Throughout the year, old wounds reopened and all my feelings of "I no longer belong here" came back with a vengeance. The hurt and disappointment piled up.

When someone shows you who they are, believe them the first time. Yes, Maya. Of course you were right.

By October 2020, I hit a new low point. Around 8 o'clock at night, I walked out of my home office after wrapping work for the day. I had a thousand-yard stare, which was fairly normal for me in those times given the hours I was keeping. As I walked into our kitchen, I looked at Colin and said, "I don't know if I can do this anymore. I feel like I have nothing left to give." I began to cry and then a deep sob bubbled up from within me.

I told Colin I didn't recognize myself and that it scared me. Normally a deeply empathic person, I could feel myself becoming numb and desensitized to those around me and what was in the news. There was more coming at me than ever before and to cope I was "sucking it up" more than ever before so that I could continue to perform at a high level. I found another gear for myself to operate in by not feeling so much.

Once happy and optimistic, I was now low-level angry much of the time. I snapped at people I loved over things that never would have set me off before.

My body showed signs of wear, too. An exhausted face looked back at me every morning. I was asking too much of my body with little sleep, little to no exercise, and far too much caffeine. I experienced not infrequent chest pains that I shrugged off (and didn't always tell Colin about because I didn't want him to worry). I also had inexplicable chronic pain for the first time in my life. My doctor couldn't find any reasonable explanation except that "it might be stress induced."

I was deeply disappointed and depleted. I had continued to hold out hope that things would change for the better, but I couldn't give the situation I was in any more chances.

After the last few years of trying to make change for myself and others, I was tired of feeling like I was throwing good energy after bad.

I was burnt out and somewhere along the way I had completely lost my sense of belonging and my sense of self. I had wanted to quit before the pandemic. By the fall of 2020, I was working harder than ever. I wasn't aligned with leadership and my sense of belonging with colleagues had been steadily diminishing for the previous three years as the culture of trust and camaraderie eroded. I felt sandwiched and powerless to make any real changes.

I desperately wanted to quit but I didn't feel like I could or should. I was lucky to have a job. I felt the (self-imposed) weight of being the primary earner in our household. I had no other job lined up and no idea what I wanted to do next. I would be jumping into the unknown. How could I quit in the middle of a pandemic? So many people had it much worse than me. How could I be so selfish?

<Deep breath> We can be grateful for what we have while demanding what we deserve.

Going with grace

I desperately wanted to quit but it wasn't until Colin said the words: "So just quit" that I allowed myself to think that was possible.

"Can I? Can I really quit?"

I wasn't willing to say "I need to quit" because that felt selfish and irresponsible. But as soon as he said it, something inside me instantly felt relief. In my brain, the person I cared about most, my partner in all things, was making it OK and "giving me permission" to take care of myself and my needs when I wouldn't do that for myself.

Thank you, Colin, for always helping me stand up for me and my needs, even when I haven't been willing to.

BUT how messed up is it that I needed that external permission and validation?! To get out of a situation that was burying me in sadness, anger, and pain?!

With Colin's words, a weight had been lifted and instead of thinking "I can't possibly quit now, I'm trapped here until the pandemic is over," I began to think "I can be free."

The next day, despite not sleeping much, I was full of energy. I started to write out a plan for how to leave in a way that supported my clients, colleagues, and myself and, hopefully, set us all up for success.

In terms of timing, it was important to me to stay on long enough to wrap up a few major projects I was leading for clients and to ensure there was a smooth transition with plenty of overlap time to shift responsibilities. I had felt the stress and frustration of quick departures many times and the feeling of being "dumped on" without enough time to properly train up others or hire additional help. We were all under immense stress and I didn't want to do that to my colleagues.

Looking at my work calendar, I decided I would give three months' notice. As with any at-will employment, it was completely within my rights to leave sooner or even immediately. I was staying on longer for my clients and colleagues but mostly I was staying on longer for myself. I wouldn't feel personally whole and complete about leaving if I didn't leave on good terms. I helped build that division of the company. I had designed the client campaigns and programs I was running. I felt a tremendous amount of personal responsibility to be a good steward of both. It was also necessary for my integrity. I wanted *everyone* in the situation to be left whole and complete from our time together.

Figuring out the practical & tactical

Before giving notice, I needed to be sure I wouldn't be leaving any benefits or money on the table.

I re-read the employee handbook and confirmed that I would need to work through the end of the year in order to get my full bonus, which was a significant part of my compensation. I would get paid out for unused vacation but only up to two weeks. At that point I had nearly five weeks of unused vacation time banked so I had to use or lose three of those weeks. I didn't anticipate that leadership would ask me to leave immediately or lock me out of my files because it wasn't that kind of company, but I needed to be prepared. I made sure that all my personal files and contacts were still mine and hadn't gotten saved onto my work server because my personal phone was also used for work.

Colin and I did the math and figured out that if I worked through mid-February like I wanted to wrap up everything for my clients and colleagues + got the two weeks' vacation payout + took my bonus without any tax withholding (so that I'd get the maximum amount of money upfront) that it would be the equivalent of continuing to get my regular paycheck through June 2021. If we cut down on other expenses, that money would go further. I figured I'd take time off and be working again by May 2020.

Minimizing harm

There's no perfect time to quit. But there are better times than others.

Everyone at my office, myself included, was on edge in the leadup to the 2020 presidential election. In addition to the (added) stress of existing as anything other than a non-white male during the Trump Administration, whichever way the election went would have a big impact on our clients. With everyone on edge, I didn't want to give notice until after the election and until (hopefully) we could all breathe a little easier knowing there would be a changing of the guard. (I wasn't overconfident about the election; I just didn't want to imagine the alternate reality.)

To prepare for when I did give notice, I put together a detailed document laying out how I recommended each of my internal responsibilities and client accounts be transitioned, how to make that work with staffing, and what timing I thought made sense based on the different client projects in motion. I wanted the other division leaders (who were also friends) to feel supported by the plan. Yes, things are going to change, but here's a way forward. Putting it all down on paper also helped me think through how I wanted to handle things with clients, people I had multiyear relationships with. There again I was asking myself, **how can they and I be left whole and complete?**

On November 13, 2020, I began to tell my closest colleagues that I was leaving. I started with the people my news would impact most.

To center myself before every call and video chat, I closed my eyes, took three deep breaths, and recited my own version of a quick meditation:

"May you and I be at peace and
may we both part in gratitude.
I am grateful for the time, the opportunities, the lessons
and the many wonderful and deeply caring people
I met along the way.
I want nothing more than for they and I to be left whole
as we part ways."

This grounded me and allowed me to hold space for whatever emotions came up during the conversations.

When I spoke to my manager and closest peers, I let them know what a difficult decision this was and how grateful I was for the chance to work together for so many years, to learn from them, and to grow together through the good times and bad.

My manager wasn't surprised at all and was very understanding because of my transparency in the year prior, given what I had shared about where I stood regarding promotion and compensation and needing to look for a new job. For me, I was re-affirmed in my choice to be transparent and upfront throughout my tenure not only because it made parting an easier conversation but also because I didn't feel any guilt or regret about not giving my employer enough chances to make it right. I quit knowing I left it all on the field.

When I spoke to my direct supervisees, three women for whom I have the utmost respect for and care about deeply, I talked about the immense joy our interactions had brought to my life and how grateful I was for their vulnerability and trust in me as a coach and advocate. My time there would end, but our relationships never had to, and I would always be in their corner.

I also asked my manager if I could be the one to tell the rest of our team about my departure because I wanted to send a direct message from the heart:

There's no easy way to say this but I am going to be leaving the firm. I am going to be taking time off to take care of myself and figure out what's next.

It has been an absolutely incredible 8+ years and I am so deeply proud of what we've built and accomplished together as a team and for our clients and the many people and causes they support. I keep a gratitude journal and I wrote this after my first week on the job:

Thank you for all the wonderful people I've met

Thank you for the opportunity to work w/ people I respect and care for.

Thank you for the opportunity to work for an organization that takes on issues I'm truly passionate about.

Those words are just as true today and those feelings and sentiments have only deepened with time. Every day I am inspired by the hard and thoughtful work you all do and camaraderie you all show each other in good times and bad. It's hard to say goodbye — really hard — but I am excited and energized for you all and what the future holds.

I was honest in responding to any questions that were asked of me, but I was careful not to bring up and rehash the anger and sadness of the past. It didn't matter now. I was moving on. I had so many opportunities to learn and grow and I learned a lot on the job that I was immensely grateful for. And now it was time to move on.

Something that was so interesting to me was that about 50% of the people I spoke with, across colleagues and clients, said some version of "Good for you, I wish I could do that." I kept thinking: "You can!" But I didn't say those exact words at the time because I had no idea what their life situation was. I did say I'd be happy to talk more about my decision and experience if folks really wanted to get into it.

I'd like to think that the me that exists today would just get into it with those people in the moment, even if it was a messy and awkward conversation. I'd dive in with: "Oh really?? What kind of change are you looking to make?" "Is there something else you're being drawn to?" "What at work does or does not energize you?" Or in the simple, beloved words of Brené Brown: "Say more."

Who knows what the other 50% of people thought. I know there were some that did and probably still do think I was absurd to walk away from a well-paying job without the next one lined up, especially during a pandemic.

Once everyone knew, it was time to line things up for a smooth departure.

I believe one marker of a good leader is that people miss you when you're gone, but the actual work doesn't skip a beat because you've been building up the folks around you all along. I strived for that ideal outcome and, for the next three months, I doubled down on building up those around me. Already incredibly capable individuals, I was glad I could give colleagues ample time to make the transition.

I will admit that once I gave notice it was harder to stay focused and give every workday my full effort. What kept me going was knowing that when I walked away, I wanted to feel like I did my best to honor my commitment to the people and I worked with and the causes I worked for. **I didn't want to feel any guilt or regret — or be left with a nagging feeling that I had left that period of my life incomplete.**

Was I ready to throw up my hands in frustrating moments? Yes. Did I say, "Are you f-ing kidding me?!" aloud to my computer in the privacy of my home office?

Absolutely. The tasks didn't get any easier just because I had given notice. What made it easier day-to-day though was to (1) breathe any time I felt anger and frustration rise in my chest, and (2) remind myself that this all had an end date. Having an end date allowed me to mentally prepare and better steel myself against the doom loop thoughts that might otherwise creep in.

Those three months flew by. During that time, I started drafting notes I planned to send to individual colleagues and my teams. I didn't want to forget anything when the time came to say goodbye.

I'm glad I gave myself that time to write those emails because it was important to me to genuinely acknowledge what an impact those people and that place had on me, and to call out the many good times we had together.

I also wanted enough time to be mindful of who I sent notes to and make sure that none of it felt like BS. I had my reasons for leaving but that wasn't important when saying goodbye. What needed to be said about why I was leaving had already been said.

In my emails I reflected on the past nearly nine years and how proud I was of the work we had all done together. There were a lot of client wins I was immensely proud of, but what I would cherish most were the times that we showed up for each other and made room for joy.

"...I will remember and cherish the deep and deeply honest 1:1 chats and the many, many, many deep belly laughs. Most of all though, I will remember and deeply cherish the ways in which we all showed up for each other in good times and bad. We've been through so much together over the past decade — personally and professionally — and those are the ties that bind. I really mean it when I say that though this chapter is ending, I know that this is in no way goodbye. I'm always just a call, text or email away and I won't be a stranger either.

Every new beginning comes from some other beginning's end.

With all the love and gratitude,
Hanah
Your friend & cheerleader"

I still get choked up reading those final emails. Not because of the Semisonic lyrics we had so often sung at karaoke nights. It was emotional because in many ways it felt like a breakup. **There was goodness there, and a lot of love, but the relationship had run its course and it was time to part ways.**

In addition to the emails I sent out, I scheduled 1:1 coffee dates and wine hours with all my nearest and dearest to be sure we didn't miss the chance to properly commemorate those last days together.

With the longer lead up to my departure, I was grateful to have created the time and space to reminisce with one another and go with grace: celebrating all that we had given each other and the permanent mark we left on each other's lives.

My work
is not
my worth.

At first, not working was easy. I desperately needed a break from work with no interruptions — something that had evaded me for most of the past nine years.

As I was preparing to leave, I reached out to a few friends who had changed jobs pre-pandemic to ask them what they were glad they did or wish they had done differently between jobs. The two best pieces of advice for me were:

- Turn off all email for at least two weeks and stick your phone in a drawer if you can.
- Get out of your house. It doesn't have to be a big trip, just take a break to get away from the norm.

I did a digital detox. I didn't read the news or social media for two weeks. I turned off my email for a month. I put time limits on my phone and began to leave it in another room for long stretches of time. I asked Colin to change his email and Slack notification noises so they weren't the same as mine and I could stop flinching every time I heard them. I didn't even realize I had that Pavlovian response!

I slept. It was truly glorious to fully disconnect and begin to rest and recover. I had work nightmares on and off since beginning my first full-time job, but I could usually still get six or seven hours of sleep per night even when I was having bad dreams. In 2020 though, my nightmares worsened, and, like many Americans, I struggled with insomnia brought on by stress. I was an early riser, usually only "sleeping in" until 6 a.m. During the pandemic I had been waking up at 2, 3, and/or 4 a.m. unable to go back to sleep. After I quit and for the first time in my life, I slept for 12 hours straight, multiple nights in a row, with no bad dreams. I obviously needed the rest.

I got out of the house. I went on a 10-day camping trip with my dad, something we had been talking about doing for a decade, but that I could never find/make enough time to do. We quarantined, packed our gear and a massive cooler with all the essentials, and drove all the way down the East Coast and back. Our most southerly stop was the house my dad grew up in on the Florida panhandle. I had never been there or heard him speak much about that time in his life. We did long walk and talks everywhere we went because we could only hang out with each other while social distancing in our "pod" of two. I learned things about my father I had never known, and I furiously took notes after our conversations so that I wouldn't forget any of what he had shared. Without digital distractions when camping and with all that time in the car, we reached a depth of conversation you just never get to when you catch up on the phone once a week.

I got to spend time with my husband. Colin works a rotating shift schedule which means that every six weeks he has a weekend or two off. During the week he may be working 6 a.m.–2 p.m., 2–10 p.m. or 10 p.m.–6 a.m. With my work schedule, I only had the weekends off and worked 7–7 most days. We were living in the same house but still missing each other, passing like ships in the night. With my time off we were able to spend time together whenever he had his "weekends," whether that was Monday and Tuesday, or Wednesday and Thursday, etc.

We began to take road trips to all the places we had been wanting to visit around New York state, staying in contact-free rentals. We walked all around a nearly empty

Niagara Falls State Park, hiked to see waterfalls in the Finger Lakes, and explored the stunning waters of the Thousand Islands.

Unfortunately, because our brains recall bad memories more easily than good ones, what I tend to remember from the vacations prior to quitting are the angry moments: getting a phone call or text in the middle of the week just when I had finally started to relax or sneaking away from my family to handle an "urgent" email request. I remembered the guilt I felt when Colin, once again, supported me working in the car while he drove the whole three to six hours to our travel destination. It pained me on one particularly long drive when he said: "Hey sweetie, you should look up for just a sec. I don't want you to miss this sunset." I didn't even know what state we were in. I had been spending time, energy, and money trying to take time off but never getting a true return on investment.

Post-quitting, **I felt more present and enriched during our one and two-day trips than I had during any of our vacations in the past decade.** I also remember those 2021 trips in much richer detail.

I worked with my hands. Once the weather warmed a bit in April, I set off to tackle as much as I could on our punch list of DIY home improvement projects. I wanted to work with my hands, continue to stay off the computer, and hopefully make another sizeable dent in our ongoing home renovation efforts. It was rewarding to see what I could accomplish with multiple days to do a project versus one to two days max on the weekends.

In just a few weeks I gave our exterior a complete face lift with all new landscaping and rock garden beds, limewashed brick, new shutters, and a freshly cleaned and painted garage door. I painted the bathroom, caulked the tub, organized the basement, deep-cleaned and painted my office, and handled all the little things I had walked past thinking "I should really fix that." HGTV would be proud. I felt capable and energized by trying and accomplishing things I had never done before. I'm not ashamed to say it also made me smile a little every time I noticed the sharp new caulk lines in our bathroom while showering or brushing my teeth.

The total pattern interrupt was a huge relief. I was still driven to be hyper productive when I did take on a new task (primarily the home improvement projects), but I was allowing myself to slow down overall, rest when I needed it, and be more present — present to my own body and feelings, and the people around me.

Accepting help

At that point, I had it in my head that I would probably be ready to start looking for a job again in May. Why May? I made it okay to not work until May because I knew that my financial "runway" wouldn't run out until mid-June. I figured that if I started looking for another job in early May then I'd be working again by the time that money "ran out." Our money wasn't actually running out. I had just done the math (and mental gymnastics) to figure out that the total money from my final check payout (final paycheck + bonus + unused vacation) was equivalent to me getting my regular paycheck through mid-June.

If I was financially covering my share then, in my head, it was okay for me to take time off. It was OK as long as I wasn't taking anything from my husband or our family or becoming a drain on our resources.

Never mind that Colin and I had had a deep conversation about finances before I quit to figure out how we could go at least a year without me working and be OK. If I did take more than a year, we would need to dip into our savings, and we wouldn't be building up our retirement at the same rate as before, but we wouldn't go into debt. He's incredibly pragmatic and wanted to be sure I didn't take this leap only to feel pressure to go back to work or take a job I wasn't all in on because of finances. He knew that is exactly something I would do — put myself and my true desires in the backseat to be sure I was taking care of my family.

Creating that space for me was also important to Colin. It was his chance to support me the way I had supported him when he changed careers.

Colin started his professional career as a Civil Engineer. By the end of his third year of college, he knew that Civil Engineering wasn't what he wanted to do, but he'd gone so far in the program that he felt he should stay the course and at least get his degree. Then he could figure it out from there.

Fresh out of college, Colin took a job as a Civil Engineer, and he too put in long hours and hard work because of the expectations he had of himself. But he wasn't happy. However, the new influx of money allowed him to do something that made him very happy: he took up flying lessons. Colin had long dreamed of getting his pilot's license after flying with his grandfather, a WWII veteran pilot and member of the civil air patrol.

During Colin's lessons he was exposed to the many people and jobs that make flying the friendly skies possible. The job that excited him most was that of the air traffic controller. They get to talk to and look at planes all day?! It was a lightbulb moment to realize he could get paid for doing a thing that truly excited him.

Sidebar: "What do you want to be when you grow up?" How on earth are we supposed to know the answer to this question?! We're literally being exposed to new types of jobs and ways to make money our entire lives. And not nearly enough of that happens before it's time to make big decisions that set us off on the initial trajectory of our lives.

Switching careers and becoming an air traffic controller would take Colin about four years. That included: going to a two-year college, passing all coursework, applying to the FAA and passing their standardized test, going to a training academy in Oklahoma City for four months, passing another series of tests to get assigned to a facility (e.g., Albany Airport), and then going through 18–24 months of training at that facility before becoming a certified air traffic controller. He had done all his research, and even with all those hoops, it was the most efficient and cost-effective way for a civilian to get into the job.

Financially, it meant taking on additional student loans, and that I would be the sole earner during the 18 months Colin was back in college and the primary earner until he was a certified controller.

In terms of the impact on our lives, it meant moving to Baltimore so he could go back to school *and* being completely flexible about where we moved to once he was assigned to a facility. It could have been Albany, NY or Bismarck, ND or literally any airport in the country that needed more controllers.

I didn't question it for a moment. Truly. It was his dream. I knew it's what he was meant to do, and I wanted to support him in every way I could to make that dream come true. I could feel it in my gut that it was the right thing for him and that this was the right path for both of us.

When we moved, I was making $57,000 a year. I got a new job and was able to negotiate a starting salary of

$75,000. The level I was hired into also had the potential for a $5,000 end-of-year bonus based on division and company performance. I was over the moon. I had complete confidence in my ability to cover our expenses while he was in school and told him as much when he would get concerned about money. "I've got you. Don't worry about anything. Just focus on school."

I didn't understand it at the time, but he still felt the need to contribute money to our household while he was in school. Never mind that he already did so much around the house so that I could work the hours I did and didn't have to take care of anything at home that I didn't want to.

While he was in school, he ended up taking on side jobs including de-icing planes at BWI Airport and working as a lab instructor at school. No matter how many times I said: "I've got this" and was 100% good to carry the team financially during that time, he still felt the need to make and contribute money — even though he was always contributing a lot to the team in time and energy.

It wasn't until I took my time off from work that I fully understood why he felt compelled to do that.

I did what was arguably thousands of dollars' worth of sweat equity work on our home and saved us lots of money through hours of research before buying anything or starting a new home project. I meal planned and cooked dinner almost every night and made meals for him to take to work. I researched and shopped at three different grocery stores to get the best prices on our staples. I also did most of the cleaning in our home.

And yet, I still felt like less of a contributor to the team when I wasn't making money.

He wanted to give me the same opportunity and freedom I had given him to figure out and go after his dreams. I only felt like it was "OK" for me to take time off when I could still cover my salary or otherwise contribute cash to our finances.

Not "OK" because I had overworked myself for 15 straight years.

Not because I was unhappy.

Not because I was unhealthy.

Not because I had given that to my partner, and they wanted to give me the same.

My brain said it was only OK to take time off when I wouldn't be a financial burden or any less of a financial contributor.

I wouldn't be *less than* because the money made me worthy of the time for myself.

It didn't matter how many times Colin told me we were financially fine (as long as we were smart and conservative in our spending) and that I should focus on taking the time and space I needed.

I had to believe it in my core that I was worthy of that time and space.

Testing the waters

At the end of April, a former colleague approached me about some short-term PR consulting work. I was thankful for the opportunity to dip my toe back in the water without a long-term commitment, and for the chance to work on my own and be completely self-directed. I honestly wasn't sure if I still enjoyed doing PR work. It was hard to separate the work itself from the baggage of the previous three years.

From the start, I tracked what about the work energized me or was depleting.

Energizing:

- I enjoyed learning about new issue areas and deep diving into related research and data (I am a proud data nerd).

- I relished the opportunity to work with smart, thoughtful subject matter experts and be a thought partner. It felt good to put our heads together and do better together, operating with a mutual respect for each other's expertise

- I loved getting to meet and coach those with lived experience who were lending their voices and personal stories to the cause. I felt useful helping passionate volunteers gain confidence in their voice and what they had to say.

Depleting:

- I went right back to checking email at all hours.

- Feeling like I should be tethered to my laptop and/or phone just in case of breaking news.

It had been over two months since leaving my job but those old bad habits and my proclivity for not setting boundaries came back real fast.

I had to set up and stick to a schedule for myself so I wouldn't hover over my laptop and phone all day. I was most mentally productive in the morning, so I blocked mornings for work and afternoons for myself and worked at keeping those boundaries.

I had some lingering bad habits that I needed to tackle *but* there were things I still enjoyed about that type of work that energized me. Given this fresh wind in the sails, I decided I should probably update my resume and begin job searching.

I stared (maybe even glared?) at the Word doc, typed then deleted on repeat, and fidgeted my way through updating my resume. My head said I *should* be doing this; my body recoiled. I was so physically uncomfortable thinking about going back to work full-time and worrying I'd end up doing more of the same old thing.

After trying for hours to make meaningful progress, I left the house to get my old trusty comfort foods. I sat on the couch, watched trashy TV to tune out, and ate my feelings with a bag of Cape Cod chips and French onion dip, accompanied by a bottle of Bordeaux.

"OK body, I hear you loud and clear. We're not there yet. Just the part-time consulting work for now. Baby steps it is."

It wasn't until June (when Colin and I were fully vaccinated) that we interacted in-person with anyone outside our most immediate family and I had to start talking about my new situation in life. We were in a mixed crowd of friends and new acquaintances, and it was the first time since leaving my job that I was asked: "What do you do?"

I was caught off guard and for a moment I didn't know what to say. Do I say I'm on sabbatical? No, they'll probably think I'm a professor. Do I say I'm a consultant? No, they might think I'm taking on new clients. It wasn't the time or place to explain my in-flux situation, so I simply said: "I'm in public relations, what about you?"

I couldn't stop thinking about that question though and I dove deep into it.

Who was I if I wasn't a Vice President? **My work was my identity. It had been that way for so long that I didn't really know who I was without a traditional job.**

I realized that somewhere along the way I had connected my value to my job. I was valuable because of what I did for others and for my ability to work hard, climb the ladder, hold the title, and make the money I did. **What value did I have now?**

Beyond my own upbringing and self-pressure to work hard and "succeed" (as defined by American societal norms), I started to wonder how much of my feelings were self-inflicted versus the result of being American. Particularly for modern women, we tend to value and praise those that can seemingly do it all, holding down a job and a magazine-ready household without breaking a sweat.

As a society we value traditional work. It's usually the second or third question in any new conversation. "What's your name?" ... "And what do you do?" Occasionally you get a "Where are you from?" before the "What do you do?" In France, it's considered gauche to talk about work outside of work. Asking "What do you do?" is a social faux pas and it's not a question at the top of the list for conversation in much of Europe or the UK.

"What do you do?" It was an innocent (and socially programmed) question, but on that warm June afternoon it opened the door for me to question what and how I thought about myself. It exposed something inside me that I needed to address: **My work is not my worth.**

And it made me realize I had more work to do on myself before I jumped into another job or whatever would be next for me work-wise. **I needed to work through old and ingrained ideas that didn't serve me.**

If my work isn't my worth, then what is? Is it the love I give and the things I do for my family? No, that's still an external validation of love. I barely had any hobbies to speak of. Cooking, reading, and the occasional hike, but should what or how much activity I *do* in any area of life really define my self-worth?

I went into a deep, sometimes dark rabbit hole ruminating on this question of worth. **I uncovered and debunked myths and stories I had been told or had told myself about worth and value as a woman, as a worker, and as an American.**

As I identified and unraveled these ideas that didn't serve me, I started to feel lighter. One by one I let them go and I began to believe something new: I am worthy because I am. I am a human being and therefore deserving of self-love. Full stop.

Then, one day, I heard a little voice inside me say: "I am enough."

I am
enough.

When it came to me, it was a whisper. Yet even as a whisper, this idea was intimidating and a little scary. That's a brave, bold place to stand, Hanah! You? Enough? Really?

I sat with the idea in meditation and let it begin to sink in. I began practicing saying "I am enough" as a mantra, in my head and out loud. Slowly, it became more comfortable to say. It no longer felt like hubris. Over time, it began to feel like both a warm hug and a shield from other's expectations and projections. It gave me inner strength and felt powerful and centering.

Yes, I am enough.

The first time I shared this idea with another human that wasn't my husband, I was scared to say it out loud. It was a close family member, and they were visibly confused. They responded with "If someone is enough, then what keeps you striving?"

It's a fair question. **To me, believing "I am enough" means that I don't need external validation to prove that I am worthy of love — love from others or, most importantly, from myself.**

Money, titles, nice things, accomplishments, and other "markers of success" in our society are not what makes me worthy of love. When I look pretty and thin, that is not what makes me worthy of love. When I give more to my family than I give to myself and reinforce the feminine ideal of selflessness, that is not what makes me worthy of love.

Being enough isn't about the things we do. It's the way we feel about ourselves. It grounds us and is foundational to being able to go out into the world and do the things we want for the right reasons. It is the pursuit of professional and personal activities for self-actualization and self-enrichment *not* acceptance, approval, and validation from others.

It doesn't mean I'm going to stop evolving or trying new things or working hard on the things I care about. It means I don't need to be hyper productive in all areas. It means I don't need to strive for an external idea of "perfection," or what I think a perfect worker/daughter/wife/woman *should* look like and be in order to be enough.

Self-actualization and the pursuit of activities that energize and enrich my life — and, hopefully, the lives of others — is *not* mutually exclusive from being enough.

Standing in the place of "I am enough" gives me the courage, confidence, and permission to pursue *my* desires and dreams instead of others'.

Let me be clear. I didn't hear that little voice in my head and "Voila!" all my problems were solved. I would love to say I never had any self-doubt or problems with self-love or feelings of "not good enough" ever again.

The belief that I am enough is not a one and done lesson that I learned and now can move on. It's a mantra and a muscle that I regularly practice and strengthen.

I have to keep working at giving myself space and grace when it comes to the process of healing and forming these new foundational beliefs about myself and forming habits that support self-love.

It is in-tim-i-da-ting to stand in that bold, brave, and very vulnerable place in support of myself. "Who am I?!" "The audacity!" But the practice of believing I am enough continues to serve me well not only when it comes to my work and career path, but also (and maybe especially) when it comes to family. It supports me in staying strong on my path and not compromising myself, my time, my energy, or my values when new opportunities, issues, or requests come up professionally or personally.

I say "I am enough" out loud *at least* once a day. And sometimes I have to say it three times fast when I see certain names light up on my phone. It's a practice, but the more I say it (and behave accordingly), the more I feel it to be true down to my core.

What does
your heart
say?

When I was 9 years old, I was enrolled in a ballet class. I loved to dance. I didn't strive to be a prima ballerina, but I thoroughly enjoyed getting to learn the moves and perform. When we lived overseas (ages 5-8 years old) I would watch MTV so I could learn the choreography in the music videos. Then, when my mom got home, I would ask her to change into her leotard (swimsuit) so I could teach her new dance routines. I would put on Whitney Houston or Tina Turner, and we would dance in the living room for as long as she would indulge me.

When we moved back to the U.S., my mom enrolled me in dance lessons. I remember being so excited to learn dance routines and choreography from a real teacher.

On the first day of class, the teacher asked us to do a series of ballet moves: foot positions, leaps, twirls, splits — all the usual stuff. She then lined us up based on how well we had done. "Look to your left," she said, "that's the person you can learn from in the class that's better than you." Everyone was to my left.

Okay, fine. I have some work to do.

I practiced all the ballet moves at home and I got incrementally better with time. Yet when I went to class every week, the teacher never remarked on my progress. She continued to rank all the kids in the class every month, putting me last. She pointedly told me I should give up because I didn't have the body type for ballet. I was heavy for my age, and I had (and have) thick, muscular legs. It was true that I didn't have the typical ballerina body type, but probably not best to tell a 9-year-old she was "too fat for ballet."

I still loved to dance though, and I was stubborn about trying to get ahead in the class. I knew I was making progress, but it seemed like this teacher was determined to keep me in my place. Finally, I got tired of the put downs. I went to my mom to let her know what had been going on and asked if I should quit the class.

Mom: **"What does your heart say?"**

When I was little and I had a decision to make, or I was facing a challenge that I had tried to fix on my own but couldn't, I would often go to my mom and ask her what I should do. She would tell me to get still and ask my heart. I didn't know it at the time, but it was her way of teaching me to trust myself and to not seek external validation or permission for my choices.

I told her I wanted to quit ballet and join the tap and jazz groups because the kids in those classes seemed to be having way more fun. And boy was I right! That teacher encouraged self-expression and joy in dance and my strong legs were an advantage for the jazz and tap moves we learned. The more I got to dance in those classes, the stronger I felt. I even lost a little weight because of the high energy and excitement that went into practicing the moves in and out of class. I was healthier in body and mind.

For all the big decision points in my life, I know I will always be better served if I get still, acknowledge and process my emotions (feel those feelings!), and ask myself "What does your heart say?" Trusting myself and my true feelings about what to choose and what's best for *me* has always served me well.

I trusted my instincts at work and on behalf of clients and others in my life, but somewhere along the way I stopped getting quiet enough to listen to myself consistently about what *I* wanted and needed. I was ignoring that my heart was unhappy and trying to tell me that things needed to change. I was ignoring what my body was telling me, too. Worse than ignoring, I was effectively telling my body to shut up and push through.

When I was reading Glennon Doyle's *Untamed* in 2020 and she talked about listening to her "knowing," I dropped the book on my lap. I knew exactly what she meant. **I wondered where along the way I had lost touch with my inner voice and tamed or silenced her with rationalizing and compromise.**

"You're unhappy." But I'm making a lot of money, and maybe that's enough. There's plenty about my life that's good.

"You're unwell." This is just temporary. I will get healthy. I'm young enough to tolerate the long hours and excessive caffeine. The workout routine starts Monday.

"You aren't aligned with leadership. You don't fit in here." But I can still do good work on behalf of others. I've dedicated so much of my life to this work, how can I quit now?

When the voice inside me had to scream to be heard in 2018, it frightened me that I was that out of touch with myself. Me to me: "If you die tomorrow, you will die with regret." Ok, you have my attention.

When I was temporarily able to adjust my work schedule and workload in 2018 after evaluating what was energizing vs. draining and making changes accordingly, I made more time for regular walks and yoga. In those moments, I began to hear and listen to my heart again. At first, she (inner voice Hanah) told me how heavy I felt but to keep going. "Don't beat yourself up about feeling heavy. The burdens and sadness you have taken on will get lighter."

I got better at my job because I created the space for stillness. From that stillness, lightbulb moments and new, better ideas emerged. Then, I backslid because I didn't maintain the schedule, boundaries, and self-discipline necessary to put myself first.

In 2019, my heart said it was time to move on. Yet I continued to rationalize why I should stay and hold out hope that things would change.

In 2020, I finally listened to myself and accepted the truths I could no longer overlook, rationalize away, or compromise on. I didn't know what was next for me, but I knew in my heart that I needed to create the space to figure it out.

Becoming a Vice President by the time I was 30 was a big goal that drove me in my 20s. I continued to strive for that next benchmark of being promoted to Senior Vice President, but I was already doing that job and I knew in my heart that the promotion wouldn't actually make me any happier day-to-day.

The gift of time off after leaving my job allowed me to reconnect with myself and listen to what I needed and desired. Instead of being driven by a master plan or big goal for what was next, I focused on exploring the next right thing for me.

The phrase "Do the next right thing" or something like it shows up in a lot in different teachings, perhaps most recognizably in the recovery community. How appropriate that it applies to all kinds of recovery and personal rebuilding?

When my head thought it was time to start looking for a traditional job again (April 2021), my heart and body said nope, not yet. So, I listened and gave myself some space.

In July 2021, after testing the waters with part-time consulting work, I thought I *should* start looking at job postings again, just to be sure I wasn't missing out. If there was something that called to me, I would try again to update my resume.

As it so happened, a role had just opened up with a prestigious foundation that I had long admired. I hemmed and hawed a bit about applying because the job wasn't a perfect fit for my skill set. It was still something I would enjoy doing though and could give me a foot in the door at the organization. I finally went for it, mentally justifying applying for the "stretch job" in a few ways:

1) I had heard and read multiple sources that talked about how "Men apply for a job when they meet only 60% of the qualifications, but women apply only if they meet 100% of them."[5] Women were no less qualified, they just took themselves out of the race before it even began. I didn't want to take myself out of the race.

2) I wanted something that would allow for continued learning, growth, and new challenges. If I had already done some version of *everything* they were looking for, how much opportunity would there be to learn and grow?

---

[5] Tara Sophia Mohr, "Why Women Don't Apply for Jobs Unless They're 100% Qualified," *Harvard Business Review*, August 25, 2014, hbr.org

3) Mom always said: "The worst they can do is say no. Then you'll just be in the exact same place you started, so it doesn't hurt to ask."

I didn't get the job. I didn't even get called for an interview.

I threw myself a little pity party. Why didn't they like me? Will I ever get a job again? Etcetera. It stings to put yourself out there and get crickets.

The job wasn't even my dream job. Yet my first instinct was to make the rejection mean something about me versus them, what they're looking for, and the many other qualified applicants that surely applied.

I allowed myself to feel my feelings of disappointment. Once that was out of my system, I was able to get quiet and practice a saying that has always helped me when I've knocked hard on a door, and it didn't open: "That's okay. That obviously wasn't meant for me." To this, I added: "If I am enough, then I am no more or less worthy of love if I don't get the job with the prestigious foundation."

It was good practice to put myself out there and test deeper waters. I was proud of myself for going after something I wasn't 100% qualified for because that meant I was overcoming past hang-ups and fears. That's a valuable lesson I walked away with! I am not a failure, and that exercise was not a failure, because it was another valuable opportunity to learn and grow.

I also realized that if I had been honest with myself and listened to my heart from the beginning, and not let any thoughts of what I *should* do creep in, I probably wouldn't have even been looking for jobs at that time. The whole process was a valuable learning experience though and it showed me I still had more self-work to do.

A significant point of taking this time off wasn't just to have a much-needed health break from traditional full-time work; it was to explore my other passions and interests to see if I wanted to make a career change. As Colin said when we first started down this path: "Write a script, go to law school, cook, go work on a woman's political campaign, whatever you want! As long as it's what makes *you* happy. I love what I do and all I want is for you to have that too."

On the bright side, the act of updating my resume allowed me to examine my career in a way that I hadn't in a long time.

In reflecting on the past and the activities that energized me most and gave me the greatest sense of joy and pride, I could see clearly that they all had something in common: supporting and empowering women.

I cherished the weekly one-on-ones and longstanding relationships I had with my supervisees. Those were precious moments when these incredible women allowed me into their lives, shared their stories and challenges with me, and trusted me to be their partner, coach, and friend in championing their careers. I was grateful for the hours I got to spend coaching formerly incarcerated women turned advocates to believe in the power of their voice and expertise. I felt fierce and unshakeable when fighting for equity in the workplace. And I felt privileged and emboldened working on campaigns to codify women's rights.

One of the things my mother always talked about with me was that she hoped that by sharing her experiences openly and honestly that I could learn from her and not have to make the same "mistakes" she had. She hoped this would allow me to accomplish more, better and faster. To her, lifting me and other women up was the greatest form of evolution in action. The way I interpreted this evolution was that it was important to understand and appreciate the struggles and lessons of the women that came before me so that I could stand on their shoulders. And, hopefully, continue the progress for myself and the women around me. Essentially, becoming part of the next set of shoulders.

Once I became a manager and supervisor, I felt a deep responsibility to share my own mistakes and lessons learned openly and honestly with the women around me so that they, hopefully, wouldn't have to go through the same. I also shared the actions, habits, and questions that had served me well in business. Not because I thought they were the "right way" to do things or there was only one way, but because I hoped it gave them a leg up as they continued to test and figure out what worked best for them in business.

Around the same time that I was reflecting on the past and the activities that energized me most, I was in conversation with two of my closest girlfriends about their own career struggles and some of the bigger questions they were asking themselves about what might be next for them. I shared what I had gone through and asked them the same questions I had asked myself about what was energizing them. I also shared my process of trying to improve things in the workplace before looking at outside options.

An idea began to form. I had more work to do on myself to be able to freely design what was next for my career and the way I best process emotions and lessons is through writing. I knew there were at least two other women like me in the world who might see themselves in and possibly benefit from my story in all its vulnerable, unvarnished truth.

The idea began as a whispered longing inside me and after a week of sitting with it, I finally said to Colin: "I want to write a book. If for no other reason, I want to write a book as a kind of therapy. But maybe, hopefully, it could help other people too, even just one person looking to make a change. I can't explain it, but this is what I feel called to do and I think I will regret it if I don't do it."

"That's awesome hunny! So go write a book." The depth of faith and love in that sentence still warms my heart.

That day, I wrote the first three chapters.

I choose me.

I made incremental progress on the book for the next four months. Why? I continued to put others first.

I knew writing the book was what my heart wanted but I didn't maintain the schedule and boundaries needed to stay in flow and keep making meaningful progress. For 15 years, my order of priorities had been my job > Colin & our home life (the "We" activities & needs) > family > me. Flipping that order of operations was taking some time.

Like I said, I still had more self-work to do.

Between Colin and I, we have three families that we love very much and are quite close to. Two on my side and one on his. We are extremely lucky in this regard, and I never want to take that for granted or waste what time we have together on this earth. I'm so grateful for all my families and all they've given to me, and that makes me want to give them all I can in return. I also put a lot of pressure on myself to make them happy and never disappoint. This is a big part of what contributed to me being the "good girl" (the good daughter, granddaughter, niece, etc.) at the expense of myself. I felt I owed them so much for giving me a good start in life that my time, energy, and money were always spent on family first. Even when I didn't have much of those things to spend.

Now that I had lots of free time, who was I to say no to family? There was also a lot going on, much more than usual, across all three families. This made it easier for me to justify putting myself last with everything that was happening with family feeling like an exceptional situation. My part-time consulting work also had an unexpected bump in activity at the end of year. It's not that I didn't want to be there for my family or do that consulting work, but I let both consume the bulk of my time and energy.

I knew what my heart wanted but I didn't set and keep the boundaries I needed for my writing time. I needed to be doing that every day — choosing *myself* every. day. — before handling family or work requests/needs/coordination/planning, etc.

I began to feel incredibly anxious to get back to me. I was frustrated and angry at myself for not prioritizing and making progress on my book and not doing things that were just for me. This was such a rare, maybe even a once-in-a-lifetime opportunity to take a break and focus on whatever I wanted for myself, and I was letting it slip away.

Remember: If I created the thing, then I can also un-create it *or* create something new.

I decided that once the holidays were over and that stretch of consulting work wrapped in December that I would be saying a polite "No" to a lot more (everything?) so that I could say yes to myself.

I was honest with myself about how I was responsible for creating the situation I was in and that doing things for others didn't just happen to me. It wasn't forced; it was the result of a series of choices I had made. Now, it was time to create something new. It was time to choose me.

I put Post-its on my nightstand and on my computer that said: "What does choosing Hanah look like today?" The first week I spent asking myself this question, the answers I got were: "Go for a walk and spend time in the woods," and "Go to a coffee shop and write." And so, I did.

Choosing me started very simply with moving my body and writing. But, as with any new habit, I wasn't "perfect" about doing it every day. Shocker! Life happened. Family requests came up. I allowed myself to be distracted by projects in the house. After all, those kitchen drawers weren't going to re-organize themselves.

At first, I beat myself up when I missed a day or two or five. But mentally punishing myself wasn't helping anyone.

I had to remember to give myself space and grace when it came to the process of healing and forming new foundational beliefs and habits that supported me. I shouldn't expect that I could quickly or magically undo 15 years' worth of habits, behaviors, and the deeper seeded beliefs about how I related to my work, my family, and myself!

I also set the bar too high for myself. Initially, because I was a historic overachiever/take-on-too-much-er, I set big, aggressive goals like "Write 6–8 hours every day!" *and* "Get in a two-hour workout!" I was just setting myself up for disappointment and more self-criticism.

I had to realize that this wasn't about "achieving," it was about forming the habit of *consistently* choosing me and doing things that energized me and made my heart happy.

Give yourself the space and grace, Hanah. Change is hard and it does not happen overnight.

I stripped down my daily routine to identify the basics of what choosing me looked like:

1) Wake up every day and practice gratitude.
2) Drink water.
3) Go outside and breathe fresh air.
4) Move my body.
5) Do something that's just for me.

I struggled with making this list at first because in my mind these tasks seemed too easy, and it felt like I was setting a low bar for myself. But the list was purposefully simple and easily achievable. It may have looked easy, but I hadn't done all five things on this list consistently, perhaps ever, and definitely not in recent history.

Wake up every day and practice gratitude. At a minimum, this is waking up and saying: "I am grateful for another day on this earth." Some days, that is all I can muster first thing in the morning. It's hard to be a human in these unprecedented times. Getting through the day and getting to live another is something to be grateful for. Saying this also reminds me that no day is guaranteed. That's not a pessimistic thought though! Thinking this way energizes and motivates me because it frames each day as another *opportunity*.

Days where I have a little more time and energy, I say thank you for all the things that support my life, working my way out from what's physically closest to me. Thank you for: my healthy body, my husband and our two sweet cats (usually all piled in the bed leaving me a sliver of space, but still, thank you), thank you for the comfortable bed I get to sleep in, the safe roof over my head, the food in our kitchen, and the health and wellbeing of our family and friends. I don't direct these statements to anyone in particular, I just put them out into the universe.

When I take the time to be thankful for the basics, my perspective shifts. I feel more energized to start the day, and everything else good that may come starts to feel like gravy.

Drink water. I used to start the day drinking two to three cups of coffee and I'd keep sipping through the afternoon. It's weird how no one told me that wasn't good for you! Just kidding (obviously). I knew it was a bad habit and steadily drinking that much coffee did all the things you'd expect it to do; it made me jittery and anxious, it affected my sleep, and it impacted my hormones and the appearance of my skin.

Now, the first thing I do after I get up is drink a glass of water. I keep water glasses and reusable water bottles around like lip balm: one on my nightstand, one on my desk, one in my tote bag, and one in the car, and I keep refilling. It's so basic but staying hydrated and limiting coffee consumption to one cup per day or swapping out coffee for low or no caffeine tea, has seriously leveled out my body. I'm more even-keeled, I have less headaches, and I get better sleep which supports everything else I want to do.

Go outside and breathe fresh air. Even if it's raining, at a minimum, I open the front door and take a few deep breaths.

I used to go days without going outside and breathing fresh air because I didn't prioritize it. I'd wake up, make coffee, start work in my home office, eat at my desk, break for dinner, then zone out on tv (and likely some wine) to fall asleep. Living in the Northeast, it's easy to become a shut-in because for part of the year it's both dark and cold out when you start and end the workday. While working from home for nearly five years, I didn't have a natural excuse to go outside like I did when I commuted into the office. I would literally have weeks where my first time going outside was to go out for dinner on Friday or to go to the grocery store Saturday morning.

Fresh air and getting outside is a huge mood booster with so many benefits, and a fairly basic requirement of being a human. It's also a great way to take a pause when feeling frustrated or overwhelmed. To take care of myself, I go back to basics and get outside to take a few deep breaths.

Move my body. Here again, unless you count walking around the house, this wasn't something I did consistently in the before times. Instead of going to extremes and saying, "I will exercise two hours every day!" I wanted to be kinder to myself and allow for flexibility depending on the day, so I simply aimed for: "Move my body." This could be a 20-minute walk, yoga in the living room, a high intensity workout, going for a hike, or dancing to a favorite playlist.

By not designating a specific must-do activity, it was easy to accomplish every day. It was also easier to get an achiever's high. With easy wins, I kept chasing that good feeling of "Go me, I moved my body today!" instead of criticizing myself for, for example, *only* getting a walk in when I had set the bar at DO A TWO-HOUR SWEATY WORKOUT! "Move my body" was also something I could stick to even when I was travelling or visiting family, making it sustainable.

Do something that's just for me. Ideally this is something that replenishes and energizes me and forwards the life I want.

On my best days that meant carving out and protecting a big chunk of time for writing my book. Getting into flow with writing was, on the whole, exciting and energizing. But, some days, after I had worked on an emotionally difficult chapter (or, let's face it, even just a few gut-wrenching paragraphs) I would feel drained. In those moments, what I needed was to take a break and turn to the other places and activities where I draw energy and inspiration: walking and listening to podcasts, reading, or wandering my favorite farmer's market or grocery store for new cooking ideas. That's right, I said walking. Some days "Doing something that's just for me" is the same as moving my body or going outside to breathe fresh air. That's OK to double up! Some days, the most you can get for yourself is just a little space and time to be alone.

Doing something that's just for me doesn't have to be a big grand gesture to self! Otherwise, it wouldn't be consistently achievable or sustainable. It just has to be something that's not about or for other people.

Is this being selfish?

When I talk about choosing me, I'm not talking about abandoning the people I love. I'm talking about taking care of myself and prioritizing my health and wellbeing.

However, in my experience, women are so often worshipped for selflessness and taking care of others that it's easy to feel selfish when you don't put others first all the time. Yet as I looked around at the men in my life, I could see that they had hobbies and things they poured time, energy, and money into that were just for them. I could see the many ways in which they protected time for themselves, and no one thought less of them for it or thought that they were selfish. In fact, people loved to ask them about their hobbies and personal pursuits. It made them interesting!

Do I look at it as selfish when Colin makes sure he gets in a workout every day or makes sure he spends time on his hobby every week? No. Why would it be selfish for me to do the same?

Do I look at it as selfish when my brother-in-law says no to a family gathering? No, he has work to do and a life to take care of. I think "Good for him for prioritizing his needs and his family."

Do I look at it as selfish when my aunt and uncle leave a holiday gathering early to go enjoy time with each other or do something that's just for them? Still no.

It's. not. selfish. I'm not talking about choosing me *all* the time, all day, every day. I'm not talking about dropping the ball on promises or commitments I've made to others. I'm talking about making sure I'm doing something for me at least once a day, every day beyond the basic life sustaining functions of eating, sleeping, and drinking water.

This is choosing me beyond the required maintenance *and* making fewer promises and commitments so that I make *and keep* time for myself.

In the before times (before my time off), I didn't think those people were being selfish, but I did feel some level of resentment in all the situations I described above. The problem wasn't with them, though. They weren't doing anything to me or keeping me from making those same choices for myself. The family wasn't disowning them or loving them any less for those choices. And no one was stopping me from carving out the time and making those kinds of choices for me, too.

Planning for success (and leaving room for life to happen)

When my job was my priority, I blocked out anyone and anything, doing whatever it took to get my work done and (over)deliver for my clients.

Yet when I was trying to make myself the priority, I was still too reactive to home/life/family and willing to put myself aside when new things popped up. When the default has always been to take care of "them" or "we" before me, it's easy to slip back into those old habits and behaviors.

I was still relating to my time, my projects, and myself as the thing that could be flexible. I knew what choosing me looked like, but I wasn't *consistently* practicing it. I wouldn't have done that to my clients or any project that I was leading. I needed to apply the same level of dedication, thoughtfulness, and planning to myself that I would to a client if I was to be my priority.

At work, the thing that had helped me most when I was trying to protect my time was to calendar out my days and weeks to give me the space to write, create, and problem solve as well as hold space for the pop-up requests and regular life maintenance activities.

Instead of reacting to the things around me and being free flow about my time, I needed to be *intentional* about designing my days exactly how I wanted.

What does my ideal day look like? What about an ideal week?

I calendared out my days and weeks in a way that matched my energy.

Daily

- My brain is sharpest in the morning (I'm a morning person) so that's when I needed to block time for writing or other activities where I'm generating new ideas and new content.
- By 2 p.m. I usually needed a break. That's when I could schedule time to move my body.
- In the late afternoon, roughly 3–5 p.m. I got a second wind and that's when I could handle correspondence (email, calls, and/or texts), pop-up requests, a grocery run, or quick home projects.
- Roughly 6–8 p.m., I wanted to protect as dinner and family time. I love to cook. It's a creative outlet for me and it's the time when Colin and I are (most

often) able to sit in the same room and talk about everything and nothing. Cooking is also a big way that I show love — to myself and to him.

- At 8 p.m. I wanted to start winding down, preferably with tea and a piece of dark chocolate.
- By 9:30 p.m. I'd be brushing my teeth then getting into bed and writing in my journal. This could include writing about my day and what I was grateful for or writing about a problem my brain was still working through so that I could get it out on the page instead of lying awake thinking about it all night.

Weekly, I needed to dedicate at least four days a week to my book writing to feel good about myself and my progress and feel like I was showing up for me. That was the minimum but, ideally, I was writing five days a week. For the other two days in the week, I wanted to protect one day to allow for play and dating my husband, and I needed one day a week to handle life maintenance items.

What are the regular life maintenance items that need to be taken care of?

I can't just let laundry pile up and ignore all things home and family so how do I fit life in?

- *Home life:* Groceries are being handled during my afternoon "free space" so what's left to tackle on a weekly basis is the laundry, my home chores (I say mine because Colin and I split and each have our designated and preferred chores), and occasionally bulk meal prep for the week.
- *Maintaining relationships:* It was overwhelming for me to always make myself available to respond to calls and texts at all hours. I never knew if a phone call was going to be a five-minute question, or a two-hour session. I love my family and I want to maintain strong, loving relationships, but I couldn't continue to operate in a "drop everything!" style when folks called. I thought hard about what would be sustainable for me and asked my parents if we could schedule weekly or every other week calls. I also let them know I would only be looking at my phone and responding to texts in the evening. Of course, if there was ever an

emergency, they could call Colin or I. Other than that, I needed boundaries and to calendar my days and weeks to better support myself and my goals.

- *Extracurriculars:* Post-vaccination and boosting I wanted to resume in-person volunteering activities. Pre-COVID I had volunteered at our local animal shelter one day a week for three to four hours. It made me feel good to do something active in my community and, short of adopting more pets, it was a way to help.

By Friday, I had typically been writing for at least four days in a row, sometimes five, so it was a good day for a break. Friday also happened to be the day that the shelter was low on volunteers, so I scheduled volunteering and all my weekly maintenance activities on Friday.

And when I say scheduled, I literally do mean scheduled. I sent weekly calendar invites to my mom for our calls. I put all my daily and weekly activities into my personal calendar to hold myself accountable, and I added them to Colin's and my shared Google calendar. He wanted to be supportive in respecting my time and space and it helped him to see where and how I planned on spending my time.

Sidebar: I can't recommend a shared calendar enough. #notsponsored Our Google calendar is the most helpful thing to be able to see and adjust schedules, commitments, and upcoming events in real time, from anywhere. It also practically eliminates the back and forth of having to ask or remind each other what you're doing when.

Blocking my time in this way not only helped me to maintain my schedule and sanity, but it also made me more present for each activity. I wasn't feeling pulled in a million different directions. Before, when I was taking calls and texts throughout the week I was almost always multitasking. Now, my parents and I talk less frequently but the conversations tend to be richer because I'm single-tasking and fully engaged.

Ok, yes, if you're on the phone with me you might hear me change over a load of laundry now and then. But I'm now far more focused and wholly present for the activities, projects, and people I care about in my life because I've thought about every single one and made each an intentional choice and commitment. I'm not in reaction mode all the time seeing if I can squeeze in one more thing.

Starting small and being kind to myself

Again, this is a practice. Choosing me started small with short walks and writing a few hours a day. I could usually keep that up for three days in a row and then I would allow myself to get distracted again for the next four(ish) days (e.g., by home projects, consulting work, researching and planning an upcoming family trip, or some other combination of we/them needs).

Setting an ideal schedule that was attainable and flexible, putting it on my calendar, and sharing it with someone else (Colin) helped me to protect my time and, slowly, get even more time back. Eventually, that three days on and four days off became five to six days on and one to two days off.

My schedule held me accountable, but I also didn't let it dictate my life to an absolute degree.

If I was in flow and inspired to keep writing, I would break for a quick walk and dinner and then go right back to my computer. If I was lying in bed and couldn't sleep because my brain was buzzing with ideas, I would get up and go write. If I was staring at the cursor forever or writing and deleting a sentence multiple times, I knew I needed to get up, move my body, get fresh air, and likely do something else that would re-energize me. Sometimes you just need a change of scene and to give your brain the space for sparks to happen.

But — and this was a key difference compared to when I started the process — **I was only flexible with my time when it came to doing *more* of the things that supported me, not less.** Whereas before being flexible meant responding and bending to outside requests and needs.

Recently, Colin asked me: "For the things that you're passionate about, do you feel like you're working as hard for yourself as you did for clients?"

Yes and no. When I was working for my clients, I was working long hours to be sure I got the job done but I was also working at the expense of myself. I see that as working very hard but not smart. Now, I am working on me with full gusto *and* preserving and protecting time to regularly take breaks and do things that refuel and replenish me so that I can keep going without burning out. I'm working hard for myself and my health.

Asking for help is hard but necessary.

I am not "Doing it all!" anymore.

When I started working a full-time job at 22 years old, I had this picture in my head of the ideal woman I should strive to be. I was a serial perfectionist and being perfect, to me, meant holding down a full-time job, working hard to get ahead, making and keeping up a beautiful home, being the good girl for my family and the only child making my parents proud, and trying to look pretty while doing it. Oh, and making it all look effortless, of course!

When Colin and I moved in together, I didn't discuss with him how we might equitably divide household chores. He was the first to bring it up. All I asked was that whoever cooked didn't have to clean up after dinner. That was the rule in my house growing up and I had always been the one to do the dishes. Now that I was an adult that loved to cook, I didn't want to have to do the dishes. That was it.

I didn't ask him to do much because I thought I needed to be the one to do everything. Perfectionism being the nasty affliction it is, I also thought all the cleaning had to be done a certain way. Which, of course, only *I* knew how to do. Colin could see that I was spending (and getting frustrated about spending) at least one full weekend day on cleaning the apartment every week. He wanted to help but he also didn't want to get in my way or mess up my way of doing things.

Then, one day, maybe five years into living together, I came home to a completely clean house. I had been out of town for a business trip that was the culmination of a difficult project and wearisome stretch of time at work. He had taken care of all the chores while I was away so that I could come home to a completely clean apartment and not feel like I had to spend any time on that over the weekend. He did that so I could just rest. I happy cried.

Were things done exactly as I would have done them? No. Did it matter? Also no. What mattered was the feeling of relief that I didn't even realize I had been missing out on. Someone else can help me carry the weight of life? OK, yes please. After that, I began to loosen my grip on having to do it all at home.

Sidebar: Thank you, Colin, for caring enough to make the bed and fluff the pillows the way I like and not hating me on the days when I can't help myself and adjust it all after the fact. I said loosen, not relinquish. I'm a work in progress, OK?

When I wasn't working at my full-time traditional job anymore, I backslid and *ass*umed that I should now take on most things at home again. I had the time so I should do it. But Colin and I had never discussed that my new job was going to be that of homemaker. My new job was to take the time and space to heal and explore what I wanted to do next.

Thankfully, he lovingly asked me to cut that shit out when he saw those old behaviors creeping back in. We did adjust household responsibilities a little bit for our new reality, but it was another reminder to not have my default be "Use your time to take care of others" and not to take things on without being asked.

Now, we each have our regular home chores. Is it a perfect split down the middle? No. But they are a better reflection of the time we each have during the week, our strengths, and preferences. I don't mow the lawn because I'm allergic to fresh cut grass. He doesn't cook dinner because I love to cook, and he prefers the precision of baking.

Whenever we need to tackle bigger projects like spring cleaning or a home reno project that I have a specific vision for, I make a shared Google doc or write out a physical list with all the steps. I use a Google doc for anything that might be repeated yearly like spring cleaning (so that either of us can access and accomplish it), and a physical list for a one-time project. I'm the planner and project manager in our team but my past tendency was to only make these lists for myself, i.e., assign myself all items on the list.

Now I make the same lists *but* before any of the work starts, we go through it together to divide up the tasks, figuring out what we can each accomplish separately and what would be easier to do together.

I am thankful to have a partner who works at carrying the load of life with me — but **it's also on me not to take on everything from the start and to ask for help along the way.**

It's like carrying all the grocery bags in from the car at once. Sure, I get an imaginary gold star for opening the front door with my hip, balancing everything, and not tripping over the cat I couldn't see through all the bags. *But* I could have taken one bag into the house, kept one hand free for the door and <gasp!> taken a second or third trip to the car with Colin. Then I would have had zero risk of hurting myself, dropping something, or bumping into one of my furry greeters.

Asking for help is still something I'm working on. As with other supportive habits I'm putting into practice, I'm unlearning 15+ years of behavior so it's going to take some time. In the case of asking for help, a good argument could be made that I'm unlearning a lifetime of behavior and conditioning. It's in my nature to carry all the bags.

I'm all about
that
good scary.

NOVEMBER 2021

Today marks one year since I gave notice. In some ways it feels like there's no way it could have been a year already and yet it also feels like a lifetime ago in terms of the place I am in mentally and emotionally. It hasn't been a year since leaving my full-time job but I'm marking the anniversary of the day I went public with my news.

It's the day when I took a stand for myself and for a different future.

It was the day I first started telling people besides Colin and my parents that I was going to leave my job with no other job lined up so that I could open the space to figure out what was next.

That day was the first time I had to face external questions about what I was doing and get comfortable standing in the place of "I don't know what's next, and that's OK."

Has it been hard at times? Absolutely. But I have never regretted my choice.

Leaving what I knew, charting my own course, and betting on myself is the greatest risk I have ever taken.

It has been *scary*. But it has been what I like to call "good scary." Good scary is challenging yourself to learn something new. Good scary is putting yourself out there knowing you could fall — but also knowing that you'll pick yourself back up. **Good scary is that feeling you get when something is wholly intimidating but also 1000% worth it.**

Not knowing what's going to happen next is definitely good scary.

What do you want to be when you grow up? Where are you going to school? What's your major? What's your job? Did you get promoted yet? When are you getting married? When are you having kids? What's your plan? What's next? What's next? What's next?

There are so many things society tells us to do directly and subliminally. We pretend like there is a "normal" way for life to progress.

When family and friends first asked me what was next for me professionally, I said I was keeping my eyes open for jobs. I said that because I thought it would make *them* feel better! Seriously, Hanah? I thought that if I said I was taking time off without a solid plan for the future that they would be concerned for me or worry about me.

I had to get comfortable saying: "I don't know what's next, but I'm excited to find out."

Once I appeared comfortable, other people (mostly) stopped appearing to be worried. Though the first time I said, "I don't know what's next, but I'm excited to find out," to a few family members the response was: "Well you'll be okay. You'll find a job eventually." I wasn't concerned, but thank you? (*So,* me trying to make them feel better about the situation wasn't entirely unfounded...)

Because of these mixed reactions from those closest to me, once I decided to write a book, I didn't tell people about it. The idea was too new, too fragile to share outside the walls of my home. I felt like this was my baby and I had to nurture and protect it. I didn't owe anyone an explanation for my life or my choices, and I wasn't going to open the door to criticism — especially when I was having a hard enough time believing in myself.

I have had to guard my heart and protect myself from being hurt by questions from the outside world about what I'm doing with my life.

It's hard not to do what people expect of you and I have questioned myself more times than I'd like to admit. I know that leaving my job and everything I've gone through since is what I needed to do for myself, but it has felt very lonely at times.

It has been painful to revisit and truly move through all the things that led me to my life change — but it was critical to feel everything and process it all so that I didn't bury and carry the pain with me. I also needed to make sure the lessons of the past weren't lost as I created a new future. Take the lessons, leave the hurt.

This experience has tested my relationship with my spouse. It has required a lot of space, grace, and trust as I've navigated the twists and turns and all the emotional hurdles along the way.

It has been hard to hold myself accountable for making change and breaking old habits as I have tested and fundamentally redefined my relationship with myself.

And yet, I regret nothing.

What's next? I don't know, but I am excited to find out. I am open to all that is possible, knowing in my core that supporting and empowering women is my calling. This book is part of that journey. I'm empowering myself by writing it and, hopefully, helping other women — even if it's just one — who may see themselves in this story.

I don't know what form my future work is going to take or what timeline it may follow. My work may even be a combination of many things.

What's important is that my life no longer has to look a certain way and I no longer have to hold a certain job title to feel as if what I'm doing has purpose and meaning.

This story isn't about quitting and finding the next thing. "Click here to see how this woman quit her job and is now making $10K a month online!" Nope. **This story, my story, is about creating the mental, emotional, and financial space to make big changes and keep exploring what energizes *me*.**

Whatever is next, I aim to live a life I won't regret.

It sounds cheesy but the only thing we can all be sure of is that we will all die. We don't know when or where, but it will happen.

There's a line I love that Jack Nicholson says in the 2006 movie *The Departed*:

"We're all on our way out. Act accordingly."

I love it because, to me, it's not morose. It's a simple, straightforward reminder.

Sitting on the carpet in our old apartment I was so scared of my own mortality because I wasn't living well. I was piling up regrets by putting myself last in the line of who and what got taken care of, and I was working hard (too hard) for everyone except myself.

I am all about the good scary I feel on this uncharted path. It is nothing compared to the scared I felt of dying with regret.

Getting my
financial
(and actual)
house
in order

Now you may be thinking to yourself: OK, that's great for you that you got to take time off but how could you afford that? I'm not a lottery winner (Yet! Still trying to manifest that...) and I'm not independently wealthy.

I was making a healthy salary. However, I was low-level frustrated much of the time about how I could possibly be working as hard as I was, bringing in as much money as I was, and still feeling like it was never enough.

Fun fact: it doesn't matter how much you're bringing in if you're being dragged down by debt. Who knew?!

Colin and I had been splitting the costs of living since moving in together, but we didn't merge finances until we got married. Between the two of us, when we added it all up, we were carrying $67,000 in debt: roughly $31,000 in credit card debt and $36,000 still left to pay off in student loans. We had to change our habits to have any chance of being debt free and to start building up our savings so that we could make whatever future we wanted possible.

I started working when I was 15 but I didn't start forming good money tracking, saving, or investing habits until I was 31.

When I was a teenager, I spent almost all my waitressing money on clothes and going out to eat or to the movies. When I started college, I put aside $500 in a savings account incase contraception failed me and I needed an abortion[6], but otherwise I didn't have any savings. In college, anything extra that I made from my restaurant hostess job (i.e., anything that wasn't used for books and school) was used for clothes and enjoying my time out in Boston.

When I got my first job in 2007, I made $32,000 a year. I paid $950 per month for an apartment I shared with two people, and I owed $200 per month in student loans. That meant half of my take home pay was already spoken for and that didn't include the cost of my phone, internet, Charlie Card, or food. The lifestyle in Boston was also very much work hard play hard, which I did. I regularly worked 50–60-hour weeks and then I would go

---

[6] I knew I wasn't destined to be a mother. It has never been my calling. Thankfully, (1) I had $500 to put aside and (2) in Massachusetts abortion was and is legal and geographically accessible.

out to dinner and drinks with my coworkers at the end of the day and go out for dinner most weekends, too.

For the nearly five years I lived and worked full-time in Boston I continued to climb the corporate and financial ladder until I made my way up to $57,000 per year. It wasn't until I made the next jump to $75,000 though that I finally started to feel like I could breathe a bit, and like there was a little extra when it came to money. I was 27 years old. I'm not even sure where that feeling of relief came from — maybe it was from not getting nervous whenever I went to the ATM. Or maybe it was the feeling of hope, like there was a chance I could get it together when it came to saving money because I no longer had just enough to cover the cost of living in a city.

Throughout my 20s I spent money I didn't really have on dining out, travel, clothes, and on gifts for myself and others.

That season of life, late 20s to early 30s, also coincided with bachelor/bachelorettes, wedding celebrations, and baby showers for our friends and family. I 1000% would not trade that time because I *loved* celebrating our friends and family! I mention it because it was easy to continue to spend and overspend on those occasions because they are all exceptional, i.e., they're not routine events. *And* it's a real financial consideration that needs to be taken into account when, as a couple, we were spending anywhere from $500-$2,500 on each wedding.

I had a *great* time in my 20s, but I wasn't intentional about my spending or saving.

Now 2016 rolls around and we're 31 years old. We each have 401K savings starting to build up, but that's it. We have all this debt, no emergency fund, and no other financial investments or assets to speak of.

We needed a real plan for creating and then holding ourselves accountable to financial goals. But how to turn this from a *should* into a *want to*? We had long enjoyed the immediate gratification of our current habits. Alternatively, **investing in ourselves and in our future had to become the thing we were excited and energized to do.**

Taking stock.

First, we had to figure out where all our money was going before we could hope to make any changes.

Enter the Mint app. This is not sponsored content, I'm just a user and believer. We had been trying to track all our finances separately using Excel worksheets and then a shared Google Sheet. When we merged finances, we wanted to find a better way to track everything. With Mint we were able to look at all our spending, categorize all of it, and continue to track spending in real time. We could see everything we spent on housing, transportation, utilities, groceries, entertainment (mainly cable, streaming services, and going out to movies), health & beauty, going out to eat, alcohol & bars, travel, weddings, clothes, gifts, and donations. There were a few other categories of spending but those were the consistent biggies.

Once we added everything up and had a clear picture of where all our money was going, we had a real come-to-Jesus moment. It's hard to grasp just how much you're spending when it's $5 here, $20 there. When you look at everything you've spent in one place, it paints a different picture from the story you've been telling yourself about how it's "not that much."

This is going to sound cliché but the one that shocked me the most was how much I had spent on avocado toast. Just kidding! It was how much I had spent at coffee shops. I had spent $3,000 on lattes. In just one year. I spent roughly the same amount of money on clothes and beauty products, too ($3,000 for the year) — and yet I still looked at my closet like I had "nothing to wear." There was also the $3,000 in 2015 that we essentially lit on fire because it went to paying our credit card interest fees.

It didn't feel great to be faced with the sum of all our financial choices, but it was critical and pivotal to face what was there. Numbers don't lie and there's no way to hide from the reality or rationalize it away when looking at a full year of choices (versus relying on how I was feeling about my spending day to day or week to week).

What value did that spending bring to our lives?

OK, so now that we understand our current reality, how do we decide what to change and how do we make *sustainable* adjustments? Where do we even start?

Colin had assembled all the numbers, but I wanted to understand how I, he, and we, *felt* about those numbers. I proposed the following questions as a guide for reviewing the year prior when it came to the unnecessary expenses (i.e., the things that we didn't *need* and weren't part of the cost of living):

- **What did we spend money on that we got the greatest return on either in terms of enjoyment, memories, or actual financial return on investment?**

- **What expenses made no positive impact? *OR* caused buyer's remorse?**

The greatest return on investment for both of us was (and still is) travel. When we reflected on the year prior, what we remembered most and what had the greatest impact were the times we got to travel together. That included *anytime* we travelled. It could have been a day trip to a new hiking spot or exploring a new town. It didn't have to be a big trip, just focused time together, away from our routine, experiencing something new and different.

Going out to eat fell into both categories. Going out to a favorite restaurant or trying a new restaurant for a special occasion held a lot of joy and good memories for both of us. I love food, food experiences, and exploring many different cuisines. However, spending money on eating out or getting takeout as a side effect of exhaustion (which was most of our fast food/fast casual spending) went into the category of buyer's remorse.

I enjoyed cooking! I knew how good it felt when I meal planned and prepped for the week and would eat most meals at home. Not making meals at home, letting groceries go to waste in the fridge, and eating out was an unseen cost of working long hours. I didn't like that I was spending the money I had just worked so hard to earn because I was too exhausted to think up and make a meal at home. Food experiences and special occasions = value. Resorting to eating out = buyer's remorse (and bloating).

Coffee was similar, at least for me, in that it fell into both categories. I enjoyed having a latte to start the day, but I was going to Starbucks again in the afternoon just to have an excuse to get out of the office and have a 15-minute break from my desk. Typically, I wouldn't even finish that second latte because it would make me jittery. Half of it went down the drain. Ugh, this is so embarrassing to type. I hate thinking back on how wasteful that was.

The point is: the first latte was part of a morning ritual that I enjoyed to start the day. (And you should get the damn latte if it brings you joy!) But I had buyer's remorse from the latte that was just an excuse to get out of the office. I was being wasteful with my money and the coffee.

I felt almost total buyer's remorse over my level of spending on clothes and beauty products. There were things in my closet I had never worn. Beauty products I had used a few times that languished in the bathroom drawers. Why did I buy these things? There were only a handful of favorite outfits and products I used and loved in regular rotation.

Then I thought back on what mood I was in when I bought those things. One of the clothing stores I frequented was next to that Starbucks I visited to escape the office. I would get my coffee and wander through the store to spend a little more time away. On some weekends, when I wanted to "escape" I would go to my favorite stores to look at the pretty things and distract myself. Online shopping was another fun distraction.

What it came down to with all these pretty things, was that I was spending a lot of money to get a fleeting shopper's high. I would also justify in person and online spending as a reward for hard work.

I am buying happiness and ending up with nothing.

I was 31 years old, making just over six figures, and working harder than ever (at least up until that point). How could I still be feeling like what I was making wasn't enough?!

Facing my finances and doing an honest, in-depth review allowed me to see that I was trying to buy happiness — and it made it easy to see all the places I was doing that. Coffee breaks, take out, clothes, Sephora, and even travel.

Yes, travel is one of the things I value spending money on and, when it's done well, it's enriching and restorative. However, I was increasingly spending more on travel and vacations because I was unsuccessful at actually *taking* the vacation (e.g., travelling to Canada so I could say my phone didn't work, booking massages hoping they would help me relax and forget about work). I was physically on vacation, but I wasn't fully present and so I kept trying more, and more expensive things to chase relaxation and mental refreshment.

By taking a hard, honest look at everything we were spending — and figuring out how we felt about all of it — it was easier to make choices moving forward that were aligned with what we knew felt

good; choices that were aligned with what we actually _valued_ spending money on.

Because I knew that errant spending on clothes wouldn't make me feel good in the long run, I stopped doing it. I started taking walks in the afternoon that didn't go by Starbucks. And, slowly, I began to form new habits around spending.

Any other necessary cost of living expenses that we could trim we took immediate action on. We reviewed all our subscriptions and made cuts to things that didn't add value or enjoyment. We moved into a less expensive apartment. When we had to buy a second car because of moving out of the city, we found an old but reliable Subaru that we could pay cash for and get a good deal on.

That year, after our first year in review discussion, we didn't set a budget. "Budget" feels like the word "diet" to us. It feels like a restriction and denying yourself something versus the mindset of leaning into and prioritizing the things that feel good.

Instead of a budget, we had:

- Two long-term financial goals:
  - Spend only on what adds value to and enriches our lives.
  - Pay off our debt in order of highest to lowest interest rate.
- A system for tracking all our spending that we could see in real time (Mint and a shared Google Sheet for the year in review discussions).
- A commitment to each other, and calendar reminders, to get intimate with our finances on a regular basis. Instead of trying to keep track of spending and trends in my head, I needed to look at my, and our, spending trends weekly, monthly, and quarterly, in addition to the year in review. When you know your numbers, you can't inadvertently lie to yourself about spending in a certain area "only" being $5 here and there. Regular check-ins kept us accountable when we started to slip back into old patterns and behaviors.
- A commitment to do the in-depth year in review on an annual basis and keep evolving our financial habits accordingly.

Getting my actual house in order

Shortly after that first year in review in early 2016, I kept looking around at all the stuff we had accumulated in our house that didn't add value to our lives and was just taking up space, and I was feeling frustrated by all the money it represented.

Around the same time, I happened to hear an interview on NPR with Marie Kondo about her 2014 book, *The Life Changing Magic of Tidying Up.* It instantly resonated with me. I went through every nook and cranny of our home at the time (a rental house that we had steadily filled up because we no longer had the natural restrictions of a small apartment).

The lightness I felt after decluttering and the goodness I felt from donating clothes, furniture, office supplies, etc. was incredible. I thanked everything that went out the door and let it go. Once we did that, it made it much easier to make good choices for us about what we bought and brought into our home. If it didn't spark absolute joy, it wasn't coming into the house.

The adjustment in my spending habits and lifestyle felt sustainable because I didn't feel like I was restricting myself. I truly felt like I was leaning into the things that brought me joy and added value

to my life. If it didn't add value, it was easy to say no or avoid it all together.

With these changes, and consciously and consistently working toward our goal of paying down debt, we managed to wipe out all credit card debt by March 2017. After that, we made a commitment to always pay our credit card bills in full so that we would never "light money on fire" again with credit card interest payments. A year later, in March 2018, we finished paying off our student loans.

Once we had paid off our debt, we felt free and able to make other investments in ourselves. Because of where I was emotionally in 2018, I regularly made comments and "jokes" about quitting. We began to talk about how, if I did need to pull the emergency eject, how could we make that work? We were in a much better financial place than we had been two years prior, but we were still living in a way that depended on two salaries.

I didn't want to be, and he didn't want me to be, beholden to my job and handcuffed by our choices if I wanted and needed to make a big life change.

We asked ourselves what it would look like to live on one salary. The biggest thing standing in the way of doing that was what we were spending on rent. The most significant change we could possibly make was to buy a house that would drastically reduce our monthly spending on housing and give us a chance to start building equity.

In June of 2019, we bought a fixer upper in a small town for $198,000. We saved up enough money to put 5% down and cover closing costs. It was not my dream house but that didn't matter. It was our starter house. What mattered was that it was a solid investment (i.e., it was unlikely that we would lose money on it) and it matched the list of core criteria we had put together: has air conditioning, is built after 1950, preferably has an open kitchen and living area, and the fixer upper projects are things we can manage ourselves (foundation and structural issues need not apply).

To say that I did not fall in love with the house at first sight would be an understatement. All I saw were projects and to dos, *but* it met the criteria. It was a house that I grew to love only after pouring hours of time, energy, and money into it over the course of three years. Now it's something that makes me smile and I feel proud of every time I see it.

I feel like an ass for writing this in 2022 when so many first-time home buyers are being shut out from affordable home purchases. The point of this though isn't to say that buying a house is the answer! It happened to be the answer for us because that's how we could most significantly reduce our fixed expenses.

The real point here is that by adjusting our expenses to live on one salary we were no longer handcuffed to both jobs *and* were able to squirrel away more money in retirement and emergency fund savings while we still had both jobs.

Then, in late 2020 when it finally came time to give notice, I was financially able to do so because of what we had done over the course of the previous five years:

1) **Assessing all our spending and what we valued.**
2) **Adjusting our spending according to what we valued.**
3) **Eliminating credit card and student loan debt.**
4) **Adjusting our costs of living to live within the means of one salary.**

As I mentioned before, I also made sure I left with the most financial runway possible, i.e., making sure I didn't leave before the bonus eligibility cutoff and getting paid out for the maximum amount of vacation days I could accumulate.

I do not include this information as a financial self-help guide. That is not my area of expertise. I include this information to be transparent about the time and financial changes that went into making this bigger life change possible.

These are the practical and tactical things done deliberately over time that aren't sexy or splashy, but that make the big, exciting life moves and changes possible. It's informative and empowering for me when people share openly and honestly about their lives, and I want to live up to that in all aspects of telling my own story.

When we sat down to do our annual financial year in review at the beginning of 2022, it had been almost a full year since leaving my full-time job (Feb. 2021). There were some remarkable and affirming takeaways.

The spending on miscellaneous shopping and clothing (aka buying happiness) had been declining year over year since 2016. However, as I grew steadily unhappier in

2019 and 2020, that spending started to go back up. *After leaving my job, my miscellaneous spending dropped by $5,000 and my spending on clothes dropped by $1,500 — both going down to almost nothing.*

Our travel and vacation spending was exactly the same as our last normal travel year (2019) but we took at least three times as many trips. We were able to do this because without my work constraints we could travel when and where the deals were, going midweek instead of on weekends and holidays when most people were usually travelling.

I didn't feel the need to take a week-long vacation to get three days of rest (knowing it would take me two days to wind down from work and that I'd start getting the Sunday scaries on Friday). I also didn't feel the need to go overboard during the trips in my attempts at escapism. We went on two- and three-day trips to get out in nature and go to places we could drive to, and I was happy just spending time with Colin exploring a new location.

Each trip also had a much greater impact on me: I felt wholly present, energized, and replenished by each and I actually remembered every single one. Those trips were adding true value to my life instead of acting as an attempted (but often failed) escape from reality.

Cell phone expenses got cut in half for a savings of $1,000. I had the pricey cell phone plan because I had to be sure my phone and hotspot would work pretty much anywhere, even internationally. Once I didn't have to be tethered to my phone, we could research other options and get a still decent but far less expensive carrier.

That's a total savings of $7,500 and we banked many more priceless memories.

As I mentioned, the year in review is a process that allows you to assess how you're feeling about and how you value what you're spending money on — and evolve based on that.

As part of our 2021 year in review, I realized that alcohol & bars and streaming services were still feeling like escapist tools that were more often used for numbing versus adding value to my life. I do enjoy a nice glass of red wine and I'm not drinking to get drunk, but the volume of consumption during and post COVID felt like something else. It wasn't alcoholism but it was unhealthy.

Additionally, as I began to ramp up the writing of this book, I was inspired by Glennon Doyle in her book *Untamed* where she talks about sobriety and feeling everything. I knew this wasn't going to be an easy process, but I wanted to feel everything. If I was to be honest, transparent, and authentic with you, my dear reader, I had to do that with and for myself too.

We have done dry January for many years now. As part of the 2021 year in review we decided to try a full year of sobriety and see how we felt. Both Colin and I have been alcohol free since January 1, 2022. It's a potential cost savings of $5,700 a year.

Money ≠ love.

The area of spending that has been the most difficult to change is how much I spend on other people.

As soon as I started making money in high school, I began getting gifts for my family. I wanted to show them I loved them and thank them for all they'd given and provided for me growing up.

Once I was out of the house and in college, I increased the amount I was spending, (even though I distinctly remember a conversation with my stepmom about how it was OK to be a broke college kid and that people would understand if I wanted to do homemade gifts).

When I started to work full-time, I instantly began spending more on gifts, as with everything else in life. I wanted to give back to my family but there was also an element of wanting to prove that I was "making it" mixed in there as well. I was the only child and the youngest in the family. I had always been around adults, I saw how they were living their lives, and I wanted to show that I was one of them and that I belonged.

When Colin and I did our first year in review in 2016, I saw that we (and mostly I) had spent a little over $4,000 on gifts for others the year prior, and that *didn't* include weddings or baby showers. It broke down to ~$1,800 spent on Christmas gifts and $2,400 spent on birthdays, annual holidays (e.g., Mother's and Father's Day), and other celebration gifts for family, friends, and coworkers.

I enjoy getting people gifts to celebrate life's moments or to help cheer them up. To me, that was a big part of being thoughtful for the people in my life. I would spend at random when I would go out shopping and see something that was perfect for Aunt X, friend Y, or colleague Z. I also enjoyed going all out at Christmas to try and surprise people. I want to show people that I care about them and a big way to do that is through gifts.

However, I was still spending money I didn't have. **I needed to make changes so that I wasn't spending on others at the expense of myself.**

I looked at my spending on gifts, working my way from the outside in:

- What was I spending on coworkers, then friends, then extended family, and, finally, immediate family?
- For each category, how did I feel about that spending? What value did it bring to my life? Was I doing it out of a feeling of should versus want? Was there any spending that had a negative impact (e.g., that I was resentful about)?

At work, I had been spending on birthday gifts and team celebrations for coworkers for years because it was something I wanted to contribute to team culture. I didn't want to stop the fun stuff but after adding it all up, I knew I needed to make changes. It was also becoming tiring to manage and I was beginning to wonder if anyone would care if I quit doing it.

I spoke to my supervisor about how we could continue these team activities but on the company's tab. It turned out I could have been expensing those things all along! I had never spoken up about it, so I didn't know that I could expense it, *and* no one had brought it up with me because they assumed I had been expensing those things to the company all along. My default was to take care of everything instead of proposing an idea and seeing if the company wanted to invest time and money into it. By speaking up, it also opened the door to rethinking our team culture activities and coming up with something new as a collective.

With long-time friends, I took a hard look at where there was and wasn't an even energy exchange. This is *not* me saying that I expected everything to be 1 to 1 with money and gifts! For me, a true gift is something given without expectation. This was me asking the question of whether, overall, friends were investing the same time, energy, and/or money into our relationship that I was. I understand that everyone is in different financial and life situations — my question was about whether they were as invested in our friendship as I was *regardless* of how that materialized.

In friendships where there was an imbalance, I stopped sending gifts and instead found a new rhythm with people of texting and calling or sending videos or a card to show love and celebrate life's moments. I took a similar approach with extended family.

With immediate family, I looked at what felt like a *should* versus a *want to* and where I could cut back or give to those family members in other ways.

For example, did I really need to bring a hosting gift every time I went to a family member's house, *or* would I be comfortable and feel like it was enough to take the time off work, fly or make the drive, help cook, help clean, do dishes, and generally support the host as much as possible during the gathering? I also realized that whenever people came to visit us, I would insist on taking care of everything while they were there because they made the trip. And yet, when I went to other people's homes, I also had it in my head that I should treat them to dinner and bring gifts because they were hosting.

Year over year, I've been able to steadily reduce spending on gifts in a way that feels good. By looking at my spending on gifts in this new way, I can still get gifts for people when I know it's something they'd love and it feels good for me to do so, but I've steadily cut out all the shoulds.

It has been a real process to face myself and my habits and unpack the unconscious beliefs behind each.

For the next act in my continued financial evolution, I'm trying to prioritize a greater focus on the gift of time.

Roughly five years into dating, Colin and I agreed to stop getting each other gifts. Instead, we agreed that we'd try to take one trip a year for ourselves and that for birthdays we'd go out to dinner. We have never looked back. I loved that instead of accumulating things in our home and feeling pressure to find a present that would one-up the year before, we got to plan a trip together. We got to experience the joy of planning the trip, taking the trip, and revisiting the memories.

As life got busier, I realized that what I really wanted from other people in my life was the gift of time. Particularly after losing dear family and friends in 2018, I was galvanized to ask my parents and in-laws about switching up our gift giving routines. I didn't want to take away their joy in gift giving if that's what made them happy, but I wanted to open the door for rethinking our "gifts" to each other. How would they feel about scrapping all material gifts and instead have the gift be visiting each other more and spending undistracted one-on-one time together?

Slowly, this has become more of the norm, but I do have to be careful that in asking for what I want and value I don't inadvertently stymie what someone else may want to do to show love or celebrate an occasion. I truly don't want to take away their joy! I also don't want to spend money from a place of feeling like I should. It's a balancing act and, as with everything, it's a work in progress.

Looking back on it all, I wish I had paid myself first from the start.

To me, paying myself first means investing my time, energy, and money in myself first and not spending those resources on things and people at the *expense* of my own financial stability and financial future.

I spent in my 20s with the mentality that I would keep making more money and that someday there would be enough to save and invest. I would work hard enough to cover my spending. *Versus,* **I am going to adjust my spending so that I don't have to work so hard forever, *and* I am going to be sure all the money I make is working hard for *me.***

In my head, somewhere along the way I had accepted that I would likely work harder and harder to climb the ladder in the same career until I was in my 50s. Then, I would take on a sunset career that was a little more relaxed in terms of hours and I would retire in my 60s.

It never occurred to me to earn and save for a career break, or to have the flexibility to switch careers, or to retire when I pleased because I had already hit the necessary savings goals. I accepted the typical lifecycle of a worker that had been established in the late 1950s/early 60s without question.

I thought of retirement and potential shifts in my career as an age-based target instead of a financial one. It wasn't until I saw stories and blogs about people like Mr. Money Moustache that it occurred to me that you could retire whenever you wanted if you saved right. That always seemed like something for lottery winners and the independently wealthy.

I and we made this career break work because of the financial shifts we made beginning in 2016 and, later, in 2019 based on the realization that I might need an emergency eject option. I have wondered if I would have felt the freedom to leave sooner if I had been prioritizing myself all along when it came to money.

Instead of accumulating things, I wish I had accumulated wealth. Primarily:

- Saving a minimum of 10% of everything I earned from the time I got my very first paycheck.
  - Particularly when I was in high school and had very few actual expenses except for my car. I wish I had begun a practice of saving *and investing* when there was so little risk so that I would have something in reserve for a rainy day, or to bet on myself as I'm doing right now.
- Saving more for retirement (so I don't *have* to keep working).
  - Maxing out my 401K every year
  - Maxing out my post-tax investments in and through a Roth IRA
- Making my money work harder for me.
  - Being an active investor. There were so many moments over the years where I thought to invest, but I never took action. I wish I had used my bonuses, back to my first $200 bonus, to invest in the market instead of buying another purse. In my head I thought of investing as something I had to wait to do until I had lots of money, versus realizing I could buy into the stock market for as little as $1 if I wanted to.

- Spending only on the things that added value to my life (e.g., time with family, friends, and enriching travel and food experiences).

Instead of, "I'll spend freely and figure out how to get by...I'll figure out how to pay for all of this someday!" I wish I had looked at what I was making, subtracted what I wanted to be saving and investing, and then figured out how to live on what was left over. Would my 20s have looked different? Probably. But I would like to believe that I still would have accumulated lots of memories (high value) instead of accumulating lots of things (lots of buyer's remorse).

Coulda, woulda, shoulda. But I'm here now. Instead of beating myself up about my choices, the best I can do for myself now is internalize the lessons and do better in the future.

Dear Hanah,

I wish I could have told you this sooner.

Dear Hanah,

You will gain so much knowledge and learn so much about yourself in the first 15 years of your career. Those lessons will be invaluable. You wouldn't become the person you are today without those jobs, those highs and heartbreaks, and the incredible people you'll meet along the way.

And yet, I wish I could have told you that traditional jobs and singular career paths are not the only option. It won't be easy, but you will love yourself infinitely more if you carve your own path.

These are the things I wish I could have told you from the start:

1. ***Your work is not your worth.***
    You are not worthy of self-love because of how much you make, what title you hold, or the number of accolades next to your name. You are a human being and therefore worthy and deserving of self-love. Full stop.

2. *You are enough.*

   Pursue professional and personal activities for self-actualization and self-enrichment — not acceptance, approval, or validation from others. You are enough and that bears repeating because it will become a mantra for you to help you stand (and stay) in a powerful place of self-love and strength.

3. *Listen to your heart. You shouldn't have to scream to be heard.*

   Make the time to get quiet and check in with yourself. You may be silencing and compromising your heart's desires without realizing it (because, for example, you're moving too fast to handle all the things and keep everything looking good on the outside).

4. *Identify and do what energizes you.*

   What energizes you or drains your energy? Keep checking in with how you're feeling about the things you're doing. Job craft and life craft to create more time and space for the activities that are energy givers and shed the energy drainers.

5. *Ask yourself: why and how did you create that?*

   If something isn't working, look at what habits and behaviors you have formed that no longer serve you. Did you teach others to expect certain things of you and/or relate to you a certain way? Take responsibility for what you have the power to change. If you created it, then you can un-create it or create something new and better.

6. *Your kindness isn't weakness.*

   Your kindness, empathy, and emotional intelligence are your greatest strengths. Don't let people tell you otherwise or undervalue that. Don't let them take advantage of you either. If they are taking advantage, they don't deserve you.

7. *Pay yourself first.*

   Time, energy, and money are the ways we invest in the people and things we care about. Make sure you have a plan for investing time, energy, and money into yourself *first* and aren't giving away all those precious resources.

8. *Remember that happiness can't be bought.*

No amount of money or things will make you happy. Money can make you feel secure, but it will not make you happy. There is a difference. Only spend money on what you value and has a good return on investment in your life. Do not fall into the trap of buying happiness (shopper's high) and ending up with nothing except buyer's remorse and a house full of stuff.

9. *Give yourself the space and grace to heal, learn, and evolve.*

Don't be so hard on yourself. Change is hard and expecting to get it right and be perfect on the first try will thwart your growth and true learning. Give yourself the space and grace to heal from any wounds, learn the lessons you need to take with you, and try again. It's not failing (talking to you, Miss Recovering Perfectionist), it's just learning.

10. *Death is certain. Act accordingly and live a life you won't regret.*

Societal expectations be f*cking damned.

Dear
Reader,...

Dear Reader,

Thank you for spending your precious time with me. I am truly grateful for it.

I cherish the moments when others have welcomed me into their lives, shared their stories with me, and allowed me to be their partner in mutual evolution. It is a true honor.

I hope that this has felt like a good investment of your time, energy, and money. I hope that by sharing my experiences openly and honestly, it may have made you feel seen, or less alone, or maybe even emboldened and empowered to make a change.

If you do think it's time for a change, I hope you give yourself a chance to listen to your heart and explore what energizes you.

You are enough. You are worthy of self-love. And you are worthy of a life that you love.

Now go find your good scary.

Much love,

Hannah

YOU ARE ENOUGH.

AUTHOR'S NOTE

I have struggled to write this while so much has been going on in the world that is gut wrenching, maddening, and demands continued action and change in the ongoing fight for equality for all human beings. I have felt guilty about taking time off and about leaving a job where I worked on social justice issues full-time. I make calls, write letters, donate, volunteer, and show up in other ways but I still yearn and aim to do more.

In January of 2021, right before I left my job, my beloved grandfather passed away. As the family writer, I offered to draft his obituary. As I sat around the kitchen table with my grandma and aunts, asking questions and typing away, it was easy to see all the love he left behind. The thought of it still brings me to tears. It was a hard but beautiful exercise of remembrance for a good man. The act of writing his obituary also made me think about what I would want written about me.

When I'm gone, I hope to be remembered as someone that deeply loved and was present for myself and the people around me. I want to be the kind of person that helps lift others and, hopefully, helps to leave the world a slightly better place than when I came into it.

But first, I needed to lift myself up. I needed to stand strong in the place of loving myself and knowing I am enough so that I could recommit myself to helping others for all the right reasons and from a place of strength.

Do I recognize that the "time off" and many of the things I'm talking about in this book are a privileged experience? Absolutely. I am infinitely grateful that I have been mentally, physically, and financially able to build a career, take a break, focus and work on myself, and begin to build something new and different for my life.

However, I don't think it's a unique experience to feel like you're on a treadmill, running fast for someone else's gain, and wondering if and how you can ever get off.

I have continued to wonder about being selfish (that dirty 's' word again) but I had to find a way back to myself and find a new place of strength within. I had to restore and replenish that original spark inside me — and learn how to stoke the fire.

What I'm finding now is that I feel resilient and better able to keep fighting the good fight because I'm taking care of myself in the ways that deeply matter.

Resources

KNOW YOUR NUMBERS

What I would keep a record of at work:

- Your job description and how you are meeting and/or exceeding it, as well as anything you're doing outside of that job description.
- The job description of the level above you and how you are meeting and/or exceeding those responsibilities and job requirements.
- Project, new business, or other wins and successes that you led or were responsible for. Ask yourself: If not for you, would that have happened? Would it have been successful?
- How much money you are managing and responsible for on a regular basis, as well as how that stacks up to others in the same position and the level above you, if applicable.
- How many people you are managing and how you have demonstrably helped them grow.
- How you are contributing to the growth of the company and employees.

- How you are contributing to company culture and any internal and/or administrative investments being made outside your job description, if applicable.
- Emails acknowledging your work and contributions to projects and people.
- Any outside investments you've made in yourself that also benefit the company and its people (e.g., diversity, equity, and inclusion trainings, emotional intelligence courses, inclusive management seminars, etc.)
- What time you are giving them "for free" (if any) *(see worksheet on next page)*

WHAT TIME ARE YOU GIVING YOUR EMPLOYER FOR FREE?

Sample from Chapter 5:

Here's a fun exercise. Take your annual salary and divide it by the number of business hours in a year. Say you're making a $50,000 gross annual salary. Divide that by 2080 (52 weeks per year x 40 hours per week = 2080 business hours). That means you have an hourly wage of ~$24 if you work "normal business hours." Now, if you worked an average of 60 hours per week x 52 weeks that's a total of 3120 business hours. A $50,000 annual salary divided by 3120 business hours = ~$16 per hour. That means you're making ~$8 less per hour on average. It also means that if you had been paid for that time, you would have made an additional $24,960. Here's the math:

3120 hours worked - 2080 avg. business hours = 1040 hours

1040 hours x $24 per hour = $24,960

Another way of thinking about it is that you gave your employer 26 weeks (1040 hours of time) FOR FREE. That's six months of work. Let that sink in. Half. Of. A. Year. that you weren't getting paid for.

TIME YOU'RE GIVING AWAY
WORKSHEET

Take your annual salary and divide it by the number of
business hours in a year:

$_____ gross annual salary (LINE A)

Divided by 2080 hours (52 weeks per year x 40 hours

per week = 2080 business hours)

= $_____ hourly wage if you work "normal

business hours" (LINE B)

Do you work more than 40 hours per week?

_____ avg. hours worked per week (e.g., 50)

x 52 weeks

= _____ total business hours worked (LINE C)

$_____ gross annual salary (LINE A, Same as

above)

Divided by _____ total business hours worked

(LINE C)

= $_____ hourly wage (LINE D)

If you are salaried and working more than 40 hours per week, what are you actually "making" per hour?

$_____ per hour (LINE D)

How much more money would you have made if you were paid for that time?

_____ total business hours worked (LINE C)

- 2080 avg. business hours per year

= _____ "extra" hours worked (LINE E)

_____ extra hours (LINE E) x $_____ per hour (LINE B)

= $_____ additional money in the bank

How many "weeks" of your time did you give away for free?

_____ hours (LINE E) worked above the 2080 avg. business hours per year

Divided by 40 hours per week

= _____ weeks of time given away "for free"

WHERE DOES THE TIME GO?

Sample from Chapter 11:

7 days a week x 24 hours per day = 168 hours

If I was getting 8 hours of sleep per night (we're talking ideal, OK?) that would be 56 hours of sleep per week.

168 - 56 = 112 non-sleeping hours per week

If I could take back my time at work and only work 9- to 10-hour days (45-50 hours per week) that would still leave me with a minimum of 62 non-sleeping non-work hours every week (112 non-sleeping hours - 50 work hours per week).

Weekend days are 13 hours long minimum if I allow myself to sleep in until 8 a.m. and go to bed early at 9 p.m. One weekend day covers the necessities: roughly 3 hours for grocery shopping and weekly meal prep, 3 hours for starting/moving/folding laundry, and the rest for cleaning the house/misc. home chores and errands.

62 non-sleeping non-work hours - 26 weekend hours (13x2) = 36 hours per work week or ~7 hours per workday (36 hours per week divided by 5 days per week) of personal time.

7 hours per day - 1 hour to have breakfast, shower and get ready every morning

= 6 hours

6 hours - 1 hour to prep and eat dinner every night = 5 hours every weekday

Rounding down to give myself conservative estimates, this math told me that *I could have at least 5 hours every weekday and 13 hours every weekend of "free time" to fill with activities that energized versus drained me.*

This math forced me to account for all my personal time and allowed me to call bullshit on my perception that there was "never enough time."

WHERE DOES THE TIME GO?
WORKSHEET

Note: This worksheet assumes 5 days of working and 2 days off every week. Adjust the numbers accordingly if you work more or less than 5 days per week.

7 days a week x 24 hours per day = 168 hours total per week

8 hours of sleep per night = 56 hours of sleep per week

168 hours total per week - 56 hours of sleep per week = 112 non-sleeping hours per week

How many total non-sleeping, non-work hours do you have available every week?

I work _____ hours per day on average

_____ hours per day x 5 workdays (on average) =

_____ avg. hours worked per week (LINE A)

112 non-sleeping hours - _____ avg. hours worked per week (LINE A)

= _____ non-sleeping, non-work hours every week (LINE B)

How many total hours do you have available on the weekend?

On weekends, I wake up at _____ a.m. and I usually go to bed at _____ p.m.

That means on weekend days I get _____ waking hours per day

Multiply that by two weekend days (x2)

That's _____ total available non-sleeping hours per weekend (LINE C)

What are the necessities *you regularly need to handle, and how much time do those take? (e.g., estimated hours needed for grocery shopping, laundry, basic cleaning & home chores)*

Hours   Activity

_____   _____

_____   _____

_____   _____

_____   _____

_____   _____

_____   _____

_____   _____

_____   _____

_____   _____

_____
Total
(LINE D)

Do the weekend hours cover all you must do *for regular life maintenance? If yes, then how many weekend hours are "leftover"?*

_____ total available non-sleeping hours per weekend (LINE C)

- _____ total life maintenance activity hours (LINE D)

= _____ hours of weekend time available

How many non-sleeping, non-work hours do you have available on weekdays?

_____ non-sleeping, non-work hours every week (LINE B)

- _____ total available non-sleeping hours per weekend (LINE C)

= _____ total non-sleeping, non-work hours ever work week

Divided by 5

= _____ total available non-sleeping, non-work hours every workday (LINE E)

What are the personal necessities you regularly need to handle each workday, and how much time do those take? (e.g., breakfast, showering and getting ready every weekday morning, and preparing and eating dinner every night)

Hours	Activity
_____	_____
_____	_____
_____	_____
_____	_____
_____	_____
_____	_____
_____	_____
_____	_____
_____	_____

_____
Total
(LINE F)

_____ total non-sleeping, non-work hours every workday (LINE E)

- _____ total life maintenance hours each workday (LINE F)

= _____ hours of time available each weekday

I could reasonably expect to have _____ hours every weekday and _____ hours every weekend of "free time" to fill with activities that energize me.

FINANCIAL YEAR IN REVIEW

Excerpt from Chapter 19:

We needed a real plan for creating and then holding ourselves accountable to financial goals. But how to turn this from a *should* into a *want to*? We had long enjoyed the immediate gratification of our current habits. Alternatively, **investing in ourselves and in our future had to become the thing we were excited and energized to do.**

Taking stock.

First, we had to figure out where all our money was going before we could hope to make any changes. Enter the Mint app. This is not sponsored content, I'm just a user and believer. We had been trying to track all our finances separately using Excel worksheets and then a shared Google Sheet. When we merged finances, we wanted to find a better way to track everything. With Mint we were able to look at all our spending, categorize all of it, and continue to track spending in real time. We could see everything we spent on housing, transportation, utilities, groceries, entertainment (mainly cable, streaming services, and going out to movies), health & beauty, going out to eat, alcohol & bars, travel, weddings, clothes, gifts, and donations. There were a few other categories of spending but those were the consistent biggies.

...It didn't feel great to be faced with the sum of all our financial choices, but it was critical and pivotal to face what was there...

What <u>value</u> did that spending bring to our lives?

OK, so now that we understand our current reality, how do we decide what to change and how do we make *sustainable* adjustments? Where do we even start?

Colin had assembled all the numbers, but I wanted to understand how I, he, and we, *felt* about those numbers. I proposed the following questions as a guide for reviewing the year prior when it came to the unnecessary expenses (i.e., the things that we didn't *need* and weren't part of the cost of living):

- **What did we spend money on that we got the greatest return on either in terms of**

**enjoyment, memories, or actual financial
return on investment?**

- **What expenses made no positive impact?** *OR*
  caused buyer's remorse?

...

That year, after our first year in review discussion,
we didn't set a budget. "Budget" feels like the word "diet"
to us. It feels like a restriction and denying yourself
something versus the mindset of leaning into and
prioritizing the things that feel good. Instead of a budget,
we had:

- Two long-term financial goals:
  - Spend only on what adds value to and
    enriches our lives.
  - Pay off our debt in order of highest to
    lowest interest rate.
- A system for tracking all our spending that we
  could see in real time (Mint and a shared Google
  Sheet for the year in review discussions).
- A commitment to each other — and calendar
  reminders — to get intimate with our finances on
  a regular basis. Instead of trying to keep track of
  spending and trends in my head, I needed to look

at my, and our, spending trends weekly, monthly, and quarterly, in addition to the year in review. When you know your numbers, you can't inadvertently lie to yourself about spending in a certain area "only" being $5 here and there. Regular check-ins kept us accountable when we started to slip back into old patterns and behaviors.

- A commitment to do the in-depth year in review on an annual basis and keep evolving our financial habits accordingly.

FINANCIAL YEAR IN REVIEW
QUESTION GUIDE

- Where did I spend money? How much and in what categories?
- What expenses were necessary? (i.e., housing, groceries, transportation, utilities & other basics)
  - Break out each line item and look at the total for each in addition to the cumulative spending for all necessary expenses
- What expenses were necessary but could be reduced?
- How much money is "left over" after the necessary expenses? (Take-home pay minus necessary expenses)
- Where did that "left over" money go? Specifically:
  - What did I spend money on that I got the greatest return on either in terms of enjoyment, memories, or actual return on investment?
  - What expenses made no impact? *OR* caused buyer's remorse?

- What did I spend (total) compared to what was "left over"? (i.e., did I really have that money to spend or was I in the red?)
- What expenses weren't planned for that I should have a plan or buffer for in future?

Then, planning for the year ahead:
- What do I value in my life and what spending do I get the most value out of?
- How could I reduce the necessary expenses?
- Where could I reduce or cut expenses because that kind of spending no longer supports what I value?
- Is there anything new I want to introduce into my life or plan for financially that I need to take into account?
- Based on all the above, what are my financial goals and commitments to myself for the next year?

ANNUAL SUMMARY SAMPLE

For your own tracking, if you don't want to go through all your accounts one by one, you can pull these numbers from an app like Mint that helps you categorize all expenses. Keep the totals in Google Sheets or Excel so you have a record of every year and can compare the totals in each category year over year to see what's changed. There are paid tools that will do this kind of tracking for you too, but there are plenty of free basic resources available. These are fake numbers, just for the purpose of illustrating this type of tracking system.

Annual Summary	2022
Income	
Salary Income (After Tax)	$57,000
Bonus Income (After Tax)	$500
Interest Income	$100
Total Income	**$57,600**
Expenses	
Rent / Mortgage Payment	$24,000
Renter's Insurance	$300
Student Loans	$3,500
Cell Phone & Service	$1,000
Restaurants & Bars	$3,000
Groceries	$5,000
Work Lunch	$750
Utilities (Gas, Electric)	$2,500
Internet/Cable TV	$1,750
Subscriptions (HBO, Netflix, etc.)	$450
Car Payment	$3,600
Car Insurance	$750
Car Maintenance	$1,500
Car Gas & Tolls	$1,500
Shopping (Clothing, Shoes, etc.)	$775
Home Supplies	$1,250
Travel / Vacation	$2,050
ATM Withdrawal	$860
Gifts / Holiday Shopping	$765
Charitable Giving	$1,000
Personal Care (Haircut, nails, etc.)	$750
Total Expenses	**$57,050**
Total Income MINUS Expenses	**$550**

A BIT MORE ABOUT THE AUTHOR

Hanah currently lives in New Hampshire with her
husband and two cats. This is her first book.
In case of typos, please blame the cats.

For the latest updates and to connect,
visit hanahsmith.com

Made in United States
North Haven, CT
25 February 2023

33168619R00178